UNIT 8

Foreign Exchange and Trade Risk

Financial Strategy

Prepared for the Course Team by Pat Sucher
and Richard Wheatcroft
with contributions from Bernardo Bátiz-Lazo

The Open University
BUSINESS SCHOOL

OPEN UNIVERSITY COURSE TEAM

Core Group

Professor Janette Rutterford, *Production and Presentation Course Team Co-Chair and Author*
David Barnes, *Author*
Bernardo Bátiz-Lazo, *Presentation Course Team Co-Chair and Author*
Marcus Davison, *Author*
Keith Dixon, *Author*
Graham Francis, *Author*
Carmel de Nahlik
Jan Gadella, *Author*
Margaret Greenwood
Heinz Kassier
Tony Anthoni, *Course Manager*
Clare Minchington, *Author*
Kathy Reay, *Course Team Assistant*
Pat Sucher, *Author*
Patricia Swannell, *Author*
Richard Wheatcroft, *Author*

External Assessor

Professor Paul Draper, Walter Scott and Partners Professor of Finance, University of Edinburgh

Production Team

Sylvan Bentley, *Picture Researcher*
John Bradley, *Design Group Co-ordinator*
Martin Brazier, *Graphic Designer*

Henry Dougherty, *Editor*
Jenny Edwards, *Product Quality Assistant*
Anne Faulkner, *Information Specialist*
John Garne, *Computing Consultant*
Roy Lawrance, *Graphic Artist*
David Libbert, *BBC Series Producer*
Richard Mole, *Director of Production OUBS*
Kathy Reay, *Course Team Assistant*
Linda K. Smith, *Project Controller*
Doreen Tucker, *Compositor*
Steve Wilkinson, *BBC Series Producer*

External Critical Readers

Stephen Abbott
George Buckberry
Linda Cinderey
Roland Davis
Angela Garrett
Jane Hughes
Ed Hutt
Rosemary F Johnson
Geoff Jones
Robin Joy
David Kirk
Archie McArthur
Richard Mischak
Professor Chris Napier
Eugene Power
Manvinder Singh
Tony Whitford

The Open University, Walton Hall, Milton Keynes MK7 6AA

First published 1999. Second edition 1999. Third edition 2000. Reprinted 2002

Copyright © 1999, 2000 The Open University

Edited, designed and typeset by The Open University

Printed in the United Kingdom by The Burlington Press, Foxton, Cambridge CB2 6SW

ISBN 0 7492 9787 5

Further information on Open University Business School courses may be obtained from the Course Sales Development Centre, The Open University, PO Box 222, Milton Keynes MK7 6YY (Telephone: 01908 653449).

3.4

26987B/b821b4u8i3.4

CONTENTS

1 INTRODUCTION

In this middle unit of the Financial Risk Management block we look in some detail at two key elements of financial risk, namely foreign exchange risk and trade risk, the latter being an aspect of credit risk concerned with the dangers of business trading, for example non-payment because of counterparty insolvency. It includes settlement risk, which can be regarded as a special, very short-term form of credit risk.

You will study 'forex' risk first – what it consists of, how to measure it and how to manage it; this is covered in Sections 2 to 7 and represents about three-quarters of the unit. The discussion also covers the main products used in foreign exchange management, with the exception of options, which will be covered in Unit 9 as a generic concept, along with their equivalents for other product groups such as equities or bonds.

The unit concludes in Section 8 with a consideration of some aspects of credit risk. Here we discuss estimating credit-worthiness but not in great detail, because your studies earlier in B821 have already given you the tools needed to have a broad understanding of credit-worthinesss. The main element of Section 8 is intended to introduce an important range of products used by businesses to ameliorate the credit risks associated with international trade (or, indeed, national trade) where supplier and buyer are hampered by a lack of knowledge about each other's financial situation. These products are called 'letters of credit' and 'letters of guarantee', or collectively 'documentary credits'. These various elements, all linked to credit risk, are referred to together as 'trade risk'.

We usually find that more students are involved with foreign exchange matters than interest rate ones at the current stage in their careers. This may make you regard this unit as more relevant to you than the interest risk material in Unit 7. While this is likely to be true at present – and we hope that will make this material of significant interest to you – it is important for you to note that this view tends to change as people get closer to the top of their particular 'tree'. Whatever the nature of the organisation, at the policy level both foreign exchange and interest rate risks must be addressed, and thus are equally important topics in an MBA finance course. And, it is hoped, the need to include credit and settlement risk is self-evident!

One point to note throughout this unit is that at the time of finalising the material (late 1998) it had been confirmed that eleven EU currencies would be succeeded by the euro in the first stage of economic and monetary union; we have chosen to anticipate the completion of this process (actually occurring on 1 January 1999) by using the euro as the currency when referring to France, Germany, Italy and the other eight participants.

Aims and objectives of the unit

By the end of this unit, you should be able to:

- use a spot currency quotation for buying or selling currencies
- calculate a forward exchange rate

- describe the linkage between forward exchange rates and interest rates
- describe some of the determinants of exchange rate variability
- calculate net foreign exchange exposure
- explain the difference between transaction, translation and economic exposure
- design a hedging strategy to control foreign exchange risk
- know where to find and how to use information for making trade credit decisions
- implement the key rules for managing the security of cash balances and funds transfer
- understand the main types of and uses for documentary credits.

Is loving the euro any easier?

2 WHAT IS FOREIGN EXCHANGE RISK?

Irrespective of the nature of their overseas activities, organisations need to understand and, where appropriate, control the degree of foreign exchange variability to which they are exposed. In order to do this each organisation must develop an organisational framework which generates answers to the following key questions.

- What is the exact nature of our foreign exchange exposure?
- How can this be identified and measured?
- Given identification and measurement of exposure, how can the degree of risk be measured?
- What is our organisation's attitude to this risk?
- How should we organise for foreign exchange exposure: centralise or decentralise?
- What techniques should we use to hedge our exposure?

This section concentrates on the first two questions. After Sections 3 to 5 which concentrate on the technicalities of the foreign exchange market, Section 6 addresses the next three questions and Section 7 covers the last question, that of how to hedge forex exposure. As you progress through these sections keep in mind your own organisation and how the contents relate to your organisation's activities.

An exchange rate is simply the price of a currency.

2.1 THE NATURE OF FOREIGN EXCHANGE EXPOSURE

What is meant generically by forex risk? It is the risk that there will be a change in value for the organisation caused by variation in relevant exchange rates; sometimes the change is represented by an actual cash flow difference, sometimes it is reflected in a change in recorded value but no funds move. This is a broad-brush definition and we need to refine it. As talked about in Unit 7, it is usual to divide foreign exchange risk into three categories of exposure: transaction exposure; translation exposure and economic exposure. We will give a brief description of the categories, and then cover each in more detail.

Foreign exchange (**FX** or '**forex**') risk was initially defined for you in Unit 7.

Transaction exposure

This is the exposure that most people would normally associate with movements in exchange rates. **Transaction exposure** arises from changes in cash flows that result from a firm's existing contractual obligations, e.g. a UK company makes a sale, denominated in euros, to an Italian company. Until the Italian company pays for the sale, there is a risk that fluctuations in the GBP/EUR exchange rate will affect the final amount that the UK company receives. Other typical types of transaction exposure are loans denominated in overseas currencies, purchases from overseas companies and dividends from overseas subsidiaries.

A guide to these codes can be found in the Glossary.

Throughout most of this text we will use the **SWIFT codes** for currencies.

Translation exposure

Translation exposure (also called **accounting exposure**) arises from the need to translate the foreign currency financial statements of overseas subsidiaries into the home currency in order to prepare a set of group financial statements in the home currency. An example would be a UK company with a Spanish subsidiary. In order to prepare the full accounts for the UK company, the accounts of the Spanish subsidiary will need to be translated into GBP and added to the results of the UK companies. Every time the Spanish accounts are translated into GBP, a uniform GBP/EUR exchange rate will be used, usually either the year-end rate or an average rate for the accounting period. Even if there were no activity in the Spanish subsidiary over a year, changes in the GBP/EUR exchange rate would mean that over time the UK translated accounts for the Spanish subsidiary could show different results when looked at in terms of the sterling equivalent. It is important to note that, though the Spanish subsidiary accounts translated into GBP may vary with the GBP/EUR exchange rate, there would be no change in actual cash flows for the Spanish company. Indeed, for most examples of translation exposure there would not be any associated cash flows in the period, since the relevant assets or liabilities would already have been in the subsidiary from earlier years.

Economic exposure

Economic exposure (sometimes called **operating** or **strategic exposure**) 'measures the change in the present value of the firm resulting from any change in the future operating cash flows of the firm caused by an unexpected change in exchange rates. The change in value depends on the effect of the exchange rate change on future sales volume, prices or costs' (Eiteman et al., 1995).

Economic exposure can be thought of as encompassing transaction exposure, but generally takes a longer-term perspective, in that it looks at the whole operation of a company and how cost and price competitiveness could be affected by movements in exchange rates. A way to see the difference between them is that transaction exposure only refers to exposure associated with cash flows that have already been contracted for (for example, sales invoiced), but the cash flows may not yet have taken place; economic exposure is much broader, covering certain cash flows (i.e. contracted for) and those which are likely to arise as the organisation goes about its business.

For example, a company manufacturing luxury cars in the UK for sale to the USA will be exposed to transaction risk on all sales to the USA denominated in USD. However, the UK company will also be economically exposed. Over time, the UK company will be exposed to shifts in the GBP/USD exchange rate. If the competitors of the UK-based manufacturer are all based in the USA, any increase of the GBP/USD exchange rate will increase its sales prices in the USA, which may mean loss of market share to local US luxury car manufacturers. You may be able to think of a leading UK luxury car manufacturer that is in this position.

Activity 2.1 _____

Review the extent to which the organisation you work for is exposed to any of the three categories of foreign exchange risk. List the areas of the organisation that are exposed to any of the categories of foreign exchange exposure, and note which currencies are involved. Keep this listing aside for a further review later on in this unit.

Let us now look in more detail at each of these exposures. As you may already have surmised, transaction exposure is probably the easiest exposure to identify, measure and cover; translation exposure is generally less important (as it has an accounting rather than a cash flow impact) and economic exposure, though of fundamental importance, is the most difficult to identify, measure and cover.

FX transactions involve the exchange of one currency for another; when selling one you *must* buy another.

2.2 TRANSACTION EXPOSURE

There are three main ways in which a potential loss or gain could occur under transaction exposure:

- if a currency has to be converted to make or to receive payment for goods or services
- if a currency has to be converted to repay a loan plus the interest
- if currency conversion is needed to make dividend payments.

In fact, transaction exposure is involved, by and large, whenever a commitment is made for a foreign currency cash flow for spot or future settlement. However, potential transaction exposure can be created even earlier than when formal contracts are exchanged, typically when a firm price is quoted but before an order is confirmed. Table 2.1 gives an example demonstrating both actual and potential transaction exposure.

Table 2.1 An example of where transaction exposure exists						
Company creates new product	Builds up stocks	Fixes foreign price for product	Receives order	Invoice date	Receipt of foreign funds	Conversion into domestic currency
		↑ Potential transaction exposure		↑ Actual transaction exposure		↑ Gain or loss due to exchange rate movement crystallised

The company designs a new product and decides to export it. It fixes product prices, builds up stocks, receives an order, sends an invoice and is eventually paid. During the whole time period between fixing the product price and actually receiving payment and converting into its domestic currency, the company is subject to transaction exposure, 'potential' at first then 'actual' once the firm order is received.

BOX 2.1 AVOIDING A CORPORATE HANGOVER

The Douro wine region

In 1995, a wine company operating in the UK imported its wines from Spain, Portugal and France. It sold these wines to high street supermarkets in the UK. As its sales were in sterling and its purchases in overseas currencies, it had a large exposure to potential exchange rate movements between the GBP and the ESP, PTE and FRF. A core amount of sales orders for the year ahead could be predicted; however, there was often substantial variation in sales of wine around Christmas and Easter each year, which were also the peak times for wine sales. Wine prices to the high street supermarkets were fixed each year in advance. Potential transaction exposure therefore arose as soon as these prices were fixed. The company dealt with this by covering 75% of the foreign exchange on its agreed wine sales, using forward contracts. At the time (summer, 1995), the company did not hedge all its foreign exchange transaction exposure as the management team felt that GBP was trading at too great a discount to the currencies above. The management team believed that GBP would strengthen against these overseas currencies and did not want to lock into exchange rates that it considered were too high.

A forward contract is an agreement to purchase foreign exchange at a specified date in the future at an agreed exchange rate. The rate is fixed when the contract is taken out so that the participants know how much domestic currency they will receive. Full details of 'forwards' are given in Section 4.3.

Note, from the example in Box 2.1, that management views of future exchange rate movements can be very important in dictating the approach the organisation takes towards its management of exchange risk. Forecasting of movements in exchange rates can therefore be crucial; it ought to be added immediately, however, that the efficacy of predicting exchange rates is by no means universally accepted. We look at forecasting in more detail towards the end of this section.

2.3 TRANSLATION EXPOSURE

Translation exposure (sometimes referred to as 'accounting exposure') arises from an organisation having assets and liabilities denominated in one or more currencies and having to prepare group accounts, that is, produce consolidated accounts. When there are foreign subsidiaries included in the consolidation, the value reflected in the 'home currency' accounts may vary as the exchange rate used for inclusion of the foreign subsidiary results alters. In this case, it is important to stress that translation involves no movement of funds between companies and, therefore, translation exposure has no direct effect on cash flow. Of course, if the organisation does actually sell its foreign assets (or repays its foreign liabilities) and repatriates the proceeds, there will be actual cash flows, but normally the business will want to continue with its foreign operations. Translation exposure, therefore, does not normally affect cash flows.

If we compare transaction and translation exposure, we can say that the former involves precisely identified cash flows and results in realised gains and losses which will affect the profit and loss account. Thus transaction exposure may have a tax effect (in that realised gains and losses are taxable or allowable against tax). It can affect all parts of the institution, and can have important future implications for the business. Translation exposure is an accounting concept which may affect future cash flows (if the relevant assets or liabilities are, at some time, realised as actual cash flows). So translation affects book values as recorded in the parent company's accounts, resulting in unrealised gains and losses which are treated as an adjustment to the balance sheet reserves of the company; this usually has no tax effect, unless and until the gains or losses are crystallised as actual transactions, for example by selling off foreign assets or paying off foreign liabilities.

Activity 2.2 ─────────────────────────────

Though translation exposure typically does not affect current cash flows, it can have some unintended consequences. Read the extract from the *Financial Times* in Box 2.2 and then consider whether your organisation may be in a similar situation to BBA plc.

BOX 2.2 BBA

BBA's decision to switch half of its dollar borrowings back into sterling looks like a perverse consequence of accounting conventions. Like others, the company had previously matched its foreign assets against borrowings on the argument that this protected it from exchange rate movements – any fall in sterling would increase the value of foreign assets and debts equally. Low dollar interest rates also kept down borrowing costs, and the practice conveniently transfers profits back to the UK to reduce advance corporation tax problems.

However, sterling's fall produces strange effects in such groups' consolidated balance sheets. Because their capital is in sterling and much of the debt is in overseas subsidiaries, any fall in the pound raises the level of balance sheet gearing. Yet provided the debt is properly matched against real business interests, and interest cover in local currencies is adequate, the gearing rise is a purely accounting phenomenon. BBA's management, however, does not want to see gearing rise any more as a result of any further fall in sterling. Hence the transfer of debt.

Its concern is understandable given the excessive importance attached to gearing. Yet crystallising a foreign exchange loss because conventions struggle to cope with the real world is the accounting tail wagging the operational dog. The Accounting Standards Board might care to look at what is clearly an inadequate method for translating foreign subsidiaries into consolidated sterling accounts.

Financial Times, *10 March 1993*

Though translation exposure typically has no cash flow impact on an organisation, different approaches to dealing with it may lead to two identical organisations, with exactly the same overseas subsidiaries, presenting different group balance sheets. Therefore if you are looking at the accounts for a group of companies with overseas subsidiaries, it is worth understanding something about the different ways in which companies can deal with the translation of the results of overseas subsidiaries.

Let us imagine a UK company with an Italian subsidiary. At the end of the UK company's financial year, it will have to translate the results (balance sheet and income statement) of the Italian subsidiary into GBP in order to consolidate the Italian results to those of the UK company. When exchange rates change, the accountant is faced with a problem of deciding which exchange rate to use for translation: the rate from the previous consolidated accounts, that current at the time of the present results or some average rate. Using each of these rates could lead to very different UK-translated Italian results. Before you imagine that all organisations can pick and choose which rate to use, there is an accounting standard in most countries on foreign currency translation that prescribes which rates to use and when. In the UK this is Statement of Standard Accounting Practice 20 (SSAP 20). Generally this prescribes, for most organisations with overseas subsidiaries, that they should translate the balance sheet of the overseas subsidiary at the rate ruling at the end of the financial year for which the accounts are being prepared (the 'closing rate'); and that the profit and loss account should be translated at the average rate of exchange for the year. This is also the approach followed by US and international accounting standards. Examples of this accounting policy are shown in Box 2.3.

BOX 2.3   ACCOUNTING POLICIES

Allied Domecq

18 Months to 31 August 1995

Foreign currencies

The profits of overseas subsidiary and associated undertakings are translated at weighted average rates each month. The closing balance sheets of overseas undertakings and foreign currency assets and liabilities are translated at period end rates. Exchange differences arising from the re-statement of opening balance sheets and profits for the period of overseas undertakings to closing rates are dealt with through reserves net of differences on related currency borrowings.

The following are the most significant translation rates to £1 at the period end and the date of these accounts:

	27 November 1995	31 August 1995	5 March 1994
United States dollar	1.55	1.55	1.49
Canadian dollar	2.10	2.08	2.02
Netherlands guilder	2.49	2.55	2.88
French franc	7.64	7.83	8.71
Spanish peseta	190	195	210
Mexican peso	11.89	9.70	4.81

Allied Domecq plc, *Report and Accounts 1995*

Thorn EMI

Foreign currencies

Transactions denominated in foreign currencies are recorded at the rates of exchange ruling at the date of the transactions. Monetary assets and liabilities denominated in foreign currencies are retranslated into sterling either at year-end rates or, where there are related forward foreign exchange contracts, at contract rates. The resulting exchange differences are dealt with in the determination of profit for the financial year.

On consolidation, average exchange rates have been used to translate the results of overseas subsidiaries and associated undertakings.

The assets and liabilities of overseas subsidiaries and associated undertakings are translated into sterling at year-end rates. Exchange differences arising from the retranslation at year-end exchange rates of:

(i)   the opening net investment in overseas subsidiaries and associated undertakings and foreign currency borrowings in so far as they are matched by those overseas investments, and

(ii) the results of overseas subsidiaries and associated undertakings are dealt with in Group reserves.

Thorn EMI plc, *Annual Report 1995*

It is important to emphasise again that translation exposure does not have a cash flow impact on the organisation, but it does affect the total balance sheet and profit figures shown in the accounts. This may therefore affect how outsiders perceive the organisation.

2.4 ECONOMIC EXPOSURE

Economic exposure is the most all-encompassing type of foreign exchange exposure, and therefore the most difficult to isolate. It relates to the exchange risk of future cash flows of the organisation. There are many different ways in which this exposure can arise. A few examples will illustrate the point.

Example 1

Apres GmbH is a German company selling skiing holidays in Switzerland to German customers. Apres GmbH faces economic exposure (as well as transaction exposure) in that, as its product is Swiss holidays and it is selling them to German customers, its future profitability will depend on the EUR/CHF rate. If the CHF strengthens against the EUR, Apres' costs will increase and, unless it can pass on the price increases, it will generate less profit.

Exercise 2.1 _____

What will determine whether Apres GmbH can pass on to its customers cost increases due to movements in foreign exchange?

_____

Example 2

Placebo plc is a UK organisation providing specialist health advice to doctors in the UK. Its main competitor in the UK is an organisation based in Germany. Placebo plc faces economic exposure. Even though it is a UK organisation servicing UK customers, as its main competitor is overseas, Placebo plc's profits might suffer from a change in the GBP/EUR rate of exchange. If the EUR weakens against the GBP, then Placebo plc's competitor will become cheaper and therefore this may affect the sales of Placebo plc. However, as noted in the answer to Exercise 2.1, the extent to which the profits of Placebo plc might suffer will depend on many issues, such as the quality of the service offered by Placebo plc compared to its competitor, the growth in the market, or customers' sensitivity to price changes.

BOX 2.4   HOTEL ACCOMMODATION

An example which illustrates the difficulty of identifying economic exposure arose in London in the early 1980s. One UK enterprise in the early 1980s provided cheap weekends in London for people living elsewhere in the UK. The cheap prices were based on obtaining discounted accommodation from London hotels which had surplus beds. This was a UK business with all cost inputs and revenue outputs priced in GBP which would not seem to be exposed to any foreign exchange exposure. However, the USD strengthened substantially against the GBP in this period, and more Americans wanted to come to London, as it had become cheaper, and these additional American tourists soaked up all the spare capacity in London hotels. The UK business therefore found it impossible to obtain the cheap accommodation it had previously obtained and suffered a dramatic decline in profits.

As the two examples and Box 2.4 are likely to have helped you to realise, identifying economic exposure to movements in exchange rates is very difficult. It is quite possible to take a 'first cut' at economic exposure and decide that a German organisation, with a production base in Germany, is exposed to changes in the USD/EUR, as sales in its industry may be denominated in USD. However, further analysis may highlight that competitors in the market are based in Japan, and even though sales may be in USD, there may be more exposure to the EUR/JPY exchange rate. You could even introduce a distinction between 'direct' economic exposure, for which the first example would be a candidate, and 'indirect' economic exposure, as shown in the second example, where the risk is very real but due more to interaction with other parties (for example, one's competitors) than the direct influence of exchange rate movements on your own cash flows.

Do not get too involved in your identification of economic exposure – for example, only use the 'direct' and 'indirect' sub-categorisations if you find it helpful. In some cases it is, but not always; it is an 'optional extra' that you should be aware of, but it is by no means crucial. What is important is that dealing with foreign exchange exposure is broader than just managing near-term foreign currency cash flows and/or local currency values of foreign assets and liabilities. It has a strategic dimension, and this is recognised in the idea of 'economic exposure'.

Activity 2.3

Revisit the notes you made about your organisation's foreign exchange exposure and consider whether you can now refine your list. How easy would it be for you to quantify these exposures?

Finally, remembering back to the first half of Unit 7, think how you would allow for and include the three types of forex exposure if undertaking a risk-mapping exercise for your organisation. This is not intended to be a deeply detailed exercise, but it is useful for you to place this very important risk category into context, and thus to gain some insight into its strategic importance within your own business situation.

In an interview on BBC Radio 4's *Today* programme on 2 July 1997, when questioned about the impact of the strong GBP on his exports, the owner of a small business which manufactured chefs' hats commented that one way in which he had dealt with the strong GBP was to move some of the production of the hats from the UK to Germany, where many of his exports from the UK were sent. This is one example of how to deal with economic exposure.

Activity 2.4

Read the article from the Course Reader, 'Operating Exposure' by Lessard and Lightstone. Throughout the article, in your mind, please replace their term 'operating' by our 'economic' when talking about exposure; both words are used, though 'economic' is more common on this side of the Atlantic (which is why we use it), so it was felt inappropriate to change the authors' preferred term.

Note how this article highlights the complexity of economic, or operating, exposure. Although many organisations might decide that there is very little that they can do about economic exposure in the short term, it is an area that has to be managed in the long term.

Purchasing power parity is further discussed in sub-section 5.1.

2.5   MEASUREMENT OF FOREIGN EXCHANGE EXPOSURE

Having identified in general that your organisation is exposed to transaction, translation and economic exposure, how do you measure the amount of the exposure?

Measurement of transaction exposure

You will probably note that Table 2.2 is very like the gap charts in Unit 7.

Transaction exposure could be measured in the format shown in Table 2.2 (a) and (b) on the next two pages. However, a decision has to be taken on how many months of sales or purchases should be included in the transaction exposure position. This varies between companies, depending on each company's pricing flexibility and how fast it can increase selling prices to offset the effect of a currency change.

Measurement of economic exposure

Economic exposure, the measure that most completely describes the company's foreign exchange exposure, is much more difficult to pin down. In order to do so, it is necessary to include both certain, quantifiable exposures and those where the risk is more strategic in nature but also less clearly defined; transaction exposure would fall into the former category, while situations such as Placebo's in Example 2 above are typical of the latter. As a result of this difficulty in measuring economic risk, organisations usually need to develop a system which can handle both hard, quantifiable data and less precise information.

One way of achieving this is to use modelling techniques, in other words to produce a 'strategic DCF model' for the whole organisation. The 'strategic' element would be that the model would be used not only to see the direct effects of exchange rate movements but also to investigate the indirect influence of currency changes through the interaction with competitors, customers and suppliers. In essence you would be performing scenario analysis based on, for example, Porter's 'five forces' model which you met in your strategy studies for B820 and in B821 Unit 2. Porter's model is not the only one that could be used, but it does consider directly the influences on one's own organisation of the other groups which are important when estimating economic exposure.

It is not intended that this 'strategic' DCF should be in any way as precise as a 'normal' DCF investment appraisal; it is intended to be a way of coming to terms with the difficulties inherent in estimating economic exposure by making use of what is now a well-understood analytical technique. The crucial thing is for the business to have a good strategic understanding of how changes in exchange rates would be likely to impact upon the organisation as a whole, and thus be able to include this knowledge in the overall policy-making decision process.

Thus, measuring economic exposure would involve 'strategic' consideration of future cash inflows and outflows, particularly the sales and marketing arms of the organisation. Then you need to 'interrogate' the model by testing it with 'what if' scenarios based, as discussed above,

Table 2.2(a) Measurement of transaction exposure. Source: Buckley (1996)

Company	US Sub Inc.	Currency	£	Prepared by	AB			Rate: $ v. £ as at 24.12.96
Country	USA	Forecast period	6 months to 30.6.97	Date prepared	24.12.96			Spot: 1.7200 1 mth 1.7300 3 mths 1.7500

	Jan.	Feb.	Mar.	Apr.	May	June	Beyond June
RECEIPTS Third party Inter-company Swedish sub	2,000	3,000 2,000	1,000	1,000			1,000 Due Sept. 97
TOTAL RECEIPTS	2,000	5,000	1,000	1,000			1,000
PAYMENTS Third party Inter-company German sub	3,000	3,000	2,000				2,000 Due Oct. 97
TOTAL PAYMENTS	3,000	3,000	2,000				2,000
NET RECEIPTS/(PAYMENTS)	(1,000)	2,000	(1,000)	1,000			1,000 Sept. 97 (2,000) Oct. 97
COVER AGAINST RECEIPTS COVER AGAINST PAYMENTS		1,000	1,000				2,000
NET EXPOSURE	–	1,000	–	1,000			1,000
DETAILS OF FORWARD COVER* (specify contract date; settlement date; rate; amount)	1.8.96 Jan. 1.7530 1,000	1.9.96 Feb. 1.7450 1,000	30.9.96 Mar. 1.7550 1,000				16.10.96 Oct. 1.7580 2,000

* Details of forward cover frequently appear on a separate schedule.

Table 2.2(b)

	Jan	Feb	Mar	Apr	May	June	Beyond June
Currencies with forward market							
EMS currencies							
Belgian franc							
Dutch guilder							
French franc							
German mark							
Italian lira							
Other EMS							
Total EMS							
Canadian $							
Japanese yen							
Swedish krona							
Swiss franc							
US $							
Others (specify)							
Total							
NO FORWARD MARKET							
Argentinian peso							
Brazilian cruzeiro							
Others (specifiy)							
Total							

Source: Multinational Finance by A. Buckley 1996

on strategic 'five forces' analysis (or whichever strategic model is chosen). Having established the key currencies relevant to the organisation, questions should then be asked about what would happen if a relevant currency changed by ±10% or ±20%, say. This then can feed into possible alternative strategies that the organisation can pursue, dependent on different currency scenarios. These strategies can cover the short term (6 months); medium term (say, 1–2 years) and long term (say, 2+ years). Currency forecasting can play a large part here (see later), and some understanding of the fundamentals determining currency rates can help, because once the different scenarios have been considered, the likelihood of the different scenarios actually occurring has to be considered, e.g. what is the likelihood that the current GBP/EUR rate will be, say, 1.45 in one year from now?

Finally, note that this estimation of economic exposure is essentially a 'qualitative' risk assessment, using the concepts from Unit 7's risk mapping. While it is expressed using numbers, particularly if you use the 'strategic DCF' method described here, it can never be more than an encapsulation of qualitative ideas concerning the risk relationships of the organisation as a whole. This should be extremely important for and useful in the strategic-level debate about an organisation's policy. Making use of knowledge about economic exposure can be advantageous, but you should always be aware of the inherent limitations of your information system.

Other risk management techniques discussed in the course use probability theory. Their conclusions are valid as long as past price behaviour is indicative of future events. See box 5.2.

SUMMARY

Foreign exchange exposure concerns the risk that assets, liabilities, profits or cash flows might change with changes in currencies. In this section you have looked closely at the three different types of foreign exchange exposure that may arise as currency movements alter home currency values: transaction, translation and economic exposure. Translation exposure is often best minimised before it even impinges on the balance sheet, for example by 'matching' foreign currency assets with foreign currency liabilities (such as loans); this will be discussed in Section 7. Transaction exposure should be identified, and a suggested approach for doing so has been presented; management of this form of forex risk will be the subject of much of the remainder of this unit. Economic exposure is more difficult to identify but, as the examples in this section have shown, it is an all-embracing form of exposure which needs to be identified and measured for the organisation's strategic planning.

3 THE MARKET FOR FOREIGN EXCHANGE

London – The capital of foreign exchange.

Movements in exchange rates affect all of us in some way or other. Whether we purchase holidays overseas, buy goods manufactured overseas or work in organisations where some of the purchases or sales are in overseas currencies, we, or our organisations, could all be affected, in some way, by movements in currency rates. Much of this impact will be in the form of transaction exposure, the risk of changes in value of transactions due to changes in exchange rates. For many organisations, though they might like to ignore them, issues of foreign exchange management need to be faced and dealt with. As I write this text (Summer, 1998) the GBP has appreciated more than 25% against many key European currencies over the last eighteen months. This change can have a drastic impact on the revenues of any UK organisation that deals with selling its services and products overseas, for example The Open University! It is therefore important to have some understanding of what makes exchange rates move and some understanding of what we can do to minimise our exposure to these movements (or perhaps take advantage of them).

This short section is intended to give you some background information about the 'who', 'where' and 'why' of the world's trading in foreign currencies. The 'how' will be covered in Section 4; doubtless you will not be surprised to discover that that section will be quite technical and will repay careful study!

In order to understand what makes exchange rates move, it is first necessary to have some understanding of the foreign exchange (forex) market, how it works, and the meanings of some of the terms used. This section and the subsequent one will not, taken together, enable you to be a foreign exchange dealer, but will give you a basic understanding of the mechanics and terminology of the forex market so that you could carry out a reasonable conversation with such a trader. One little point: as exchange rates can change so rapidly, the rates we use in this text may seem out of date by the time you read this text. The mechanics will, however, be the same.

3.1   WHAT AND WHERE IS THE FOREIGN EXCHANGE MARKET?

The **foreign exchange market** is the organisational framework within which individuals, companies, banks and brokers buy and sell foreign currencies. The foreign exchange market for any one currency such as the GBP consists of all the locations such as London, New York, Frankfurt and Tokyo where the GBP is bought and sold for other currencies. The foreign exchange market consists of two levels: the interbank or 'wholesale' market, and the client or 'retail' market. Transactions in the interbank market are for large amounts of currency (e.g. several million USD). Transactions in the retail market are usually for smaller amounts. Note, however, that this distinction between 'wholesale' and 'retail' is no more hard-and-fast than it is in our everyday shopping for goods and services: if you are able to do transactions in wholesale quantities and follow appropriate custom and practice, you can usually obtain wholesale pricing whether you are really a 'customer' or a 'wholesaler'.

You may ask, where do you find wholesale transactions in foreign exchange? Well, first, you are likely to find them in your country's capital or main local financial centre. This is because the major market for any single currency is its home country and, therefore, the greatest demand for this type of service is the city where most foreign trade takes place. A second type of market for wholesale currency trade is the network of local banks, international banks and multinational companies. These trades link national financial centres and global financial centres. For example, Prague, Madrid and Mexico City are national financial centres. They are the major centres to exchange local currency for hard currency transactions or vice versa. They are also the main centres for local securities and home government bonds. Finally, the third type of market is found only in London, New York and Tokyo or the three global financial centres. These centres support the international interbank market.

Despite time and space differences, there exists the possibility to trade any time of day or night in the international and global foreign exchange markets. This is because participants – called foreign exchange brokers or FX dealers – form an electronically linked network, whose purpose is to facilitate the efficient operation of the FX market by bringing together those who wish to trade in currencies.

Foreign exchange brokers deal with banks, local and multinational businesses, governments and supra-national organisations. But, of course, most banks own and manage a foreign exchange broker/dealer.

Banks in Asia Pacific begin trading in Hong Kong, Singapore and Tokyo at about the time most traders in San Francisco are finishing. As Asia Pacific closes, trading in the Middle Eastern financial centres has been going on for two hours, and the trading day in Europe is just beginning. The continuous overlap of foreign exchange trading in different centres is illustrated in Figure 3.1 opposite. Due to the UK's geographical location, banks in London can deal with Asia Pacific, the Middle East and the USA, as well as with the rest of Europe, during a working day. This has helped London to maintain a pre-eminent position in the foreign exchange market.

Activity 3.1

Clearly, European economic and monetary union ('EMU'), especially the introduction of the euro, will be a crucial factor in the financial environment throughout the life of B821. Thus, while it is important for you to include the topic in your studies, the situation is changing so rapidly as to make it impractical to print material here in the core unit – articles would be old long before they reached you.

 We have therefore placed appropriate current material about the debate and application of EMU on the course website; this will be reviewed and, where necessary, updated by the Course Team on a regular basis. Please inspect the material provided for your presentation of the course. You are not required to read all of it in depth, but are expected to have or to acquire a basic understanding of the key factors of EMU and the euro, plus a general knowledge of 'the state of play' at the time of your study of B821.

3.2   THE SIZE OF THE WORLD CURRENCY MARKETS

Strictly speaking, the report refers to the UK, USA and Japan, but the three cities account for the vast majority of the respective totals.

Every three years, the Bank for International Settlements (BIS), in conjunction with the central banks throughout the world, publishes a survey of global net turnover in currency trading. Global net turnover means the total USD value of all spot, outright forward, swap, futures and options contracts concluded. The most recent survey, conducted in April 1998, estimated global net turnover in the world foreign exchange markets as USD1,490 billion per working day. This had grown by 25% from USD1,190 billion when the previous survey was published in 1995. To put these amounts in perspective, figures from the International Monetary Fund for 1994 indicate that the total volume of goods and services traded in the world was USD4,314.9 billion – a mere 3.5 days of activity on the foreign exchanges. London, New York and Tokyo accounted for 58% of all world foreign exchange turnover. London was the largest foreign exchange market with 32% of the total world market. Particular features of the London market were that, of the USD637 billion turnover, USD217 billion was

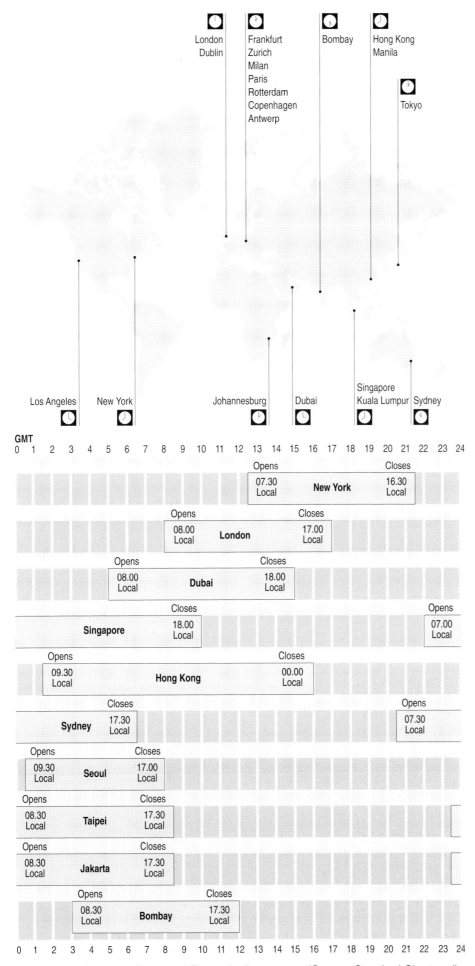

Figure 3.1   Standard Chartered Group dealing centres (Source: Standard Chartered)

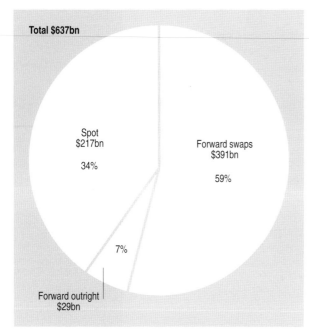

Figure 3.2   London forex market: 1998 figures

in spot transactions and USD420 billion in the forward market (of which nearly 90% were swap transactions); this is summarised in Figure 3.2. Almost 90% of all foreign exchange activity in London involved the US dollar, with the USD/DEM (remember, at the time it was the Deutschmark, not the euro) dominating with 22% of transactions. 83% of the trading was in the interbank market.

Exercise 3.1

What do you think are the implications of 83% of trading in foreign exchange being in the interbank market rather than between corporates and banks?

3.3   WHY AND FOR WHOM DOES THE FOREX MARKET EXIST?

Answering the 'why' first, it exists because the world's economic system is built upon a large number of different currencies, many of which people and organisations are legally permitted to buy and sell – the 'freely convertible' currencies. Without such currencies, or just one single 'world currency', settlement for trade between nations would be extremely difficult; indeed, the extreme position would require a return to barter for international trade!

Note the system does not require all currencies to be 'freely convertible', only that a medium of exchange is available. Thus the old Soviet Union's rouble, the Chinese renmimbi and the currencies of some smaller nations were or are said to be 'non-convertible'; in fact they are convertible, but you can only do so through the appropriate government, subject to its restraints and terms. This does not always prevent a clandestine 'free market' developing in parallel, especially where government terms are unrealistic.

BOX 3.1   THE MARKET FOR FOREIGN EXCHANGE

According to the International Monetary Fund (IMF) in 1995 there were 141 currencies in the world. This means that any one currency could be priced 140 times or have 140 markets to buy or sell the home currency. In order words,

141 currencies * 140   = 19,740 currency cross-rates.

For reasons that will be evident below, there must be a symmetry between the amount of currency 'A' paid in exchange for currency 'B'. That is to say, that in any particular moment in time, the amount of Japanese yens to be paid for an Australian dollar (¥ 62.5 = A$1.00) should be equal to the inverse of the amount of Australian dollars to be paid for a Japanese yen (¥ 1 = A$0.016). Therefore,

19,740 currency cross-rates / 2 = 9,870 exchange rates.

However, the actual number of exchange rates is a little bit lower than the one shown above. This is because some countries do not engage in international trade, such as North Korea or Iraq. Formally, it is said that not all currencies in the world are *convertible*. Non-convertibility means that either monetary authorities have imposed exchange controls or that the foreign trade of the country is relatively small and, therefore, that the country's currency will not be exchanged (and hence priced) in all currency markets.

For example, the government of the Peoples Republic of China maintains exchange control and refuses conversion of external Chinese renmimbi balances. So there is no external exchange trading. Similarly, with little trade between Singapore and Romania, the Romanians find it uninteresting to price Singapore dollars, although the Singapore dollar is very actively traded throughout East Asia.

Nonetheless, the number of currencies to be priced will still be considerable and the actual number changes each year (as international trade flows are ever increasing). Note, however, that households and firms involved in international trade do not engage in buying and selling foreign currency directly. Rather they work through a bank which will, in turn, work through a foreign exchange broker.

Source: Wood and Bátiz-Lazo (1995)

Thus the existence of the forex market is necessary for international trade and movement, but you should also note, as was seen in the preceding sub-section, that the size of the actual market is much bigger than would be the case if trade transactions alone were involved.

The participants in the foreign currency market can be categorised as:

- traders in goods and services (i.e. importers and exporters and multinational companies)
- investors
- recipients and payers of dividends, interest, profits, royalties and loans
- speculators
- arbitrageurs
- central banks.

A **speculator** is, in this context, a currency trader whose purpose is not to hedge an underlying financial exposure but to take calculated risks on market prices for profit. An **arbitrageur** is an individual who seeks to obtain risk-free profits in a trading situation by taking advantage of pricing differences for the same product. An arbitrageur 'arbitrages away' the difference by buying and selling the same item at the different prices in different markets. As noted in the statistics above, most of the trading is in the interbank market. Banks are acting in the interbank market on their own behalf and on behalf of their customers. The customers comprise central banks, foreign banks, governments, companies and individuals who wish to dispose of or acquire an amount of money from the bank in a particular currency. However, only a small fraction of the total volume of daily business in currency is on behalf of customers wishing to finance their trading and capital flows; the vast bulk of all currency business is between the banks themselves.

You have already come across the ideas of arbitrage, but they will be particularly important for understanding parts of Section 4.

SUMMARY

In this section you have looked in a general way at the 'who', 'where' and 'why' of the world's trading in foreign currencies. The foreign exchange market consists of two levels: the 'wholesale' and the 'retail' level, and the difference between the two is mainly the size of the transactions. The foreign exchange market is not a physical place, but an electronically linked network of institutions such as banks. The market is extremely large and exists to provide currency convertibility to enable international trade and movement. However, the great majority of foreign exchange transactions are for speculation and arbitrage. In the next section we will look more closely at the details of trading in the currency markets.

4 THE MECHANICS OF FOREIGN EXCHANGE

In this section you will get to grips with the core technical material of this unit. We will start by looking at spot rates, which are deals done for settlement 'now' – strictly speaking, in two working days, but the delay is for processing rather than conceptual reasons. You have already met the idea of 'spot' as two days in the future when considering 'gap charts' in Unit 7, and you have also been warned later on in the same unit that 'spot interest rates' are different creatures from 'spot exchange rates'. Which one is being used at any one time is clear from the context, and you may assume that for the rest of this unit we are talking foreign exchange whenever we use the term 'spot rate'.

The section continues with a discussion of cross rates; these may be spot rates or forward rates but are needed whenever we want to deal currency A against currency B, but each is only quoted against currency C. In other words we have a rate for A against C and B against C but need to calculate A against B. Replace C with 'US dollar' and you may begin to see why you need to learn about cross rates: in the real world, almost all currencies at least have an exchange rate quoted against the dollar.

A major topic for this section is **forward exchange rates**, and we will see that in reality a forward exchange rate can be thought of as a spot rate adjusted for the fact that delivery will be delayed until a known date in the future. Perhaps surprisingly, a forward exchange rate is not the market result of trying to forecast what the actual exchange rate will be in one or three or six months' time; it is defined exactly by an 'arbitrage relationship' based on the cost of delaying settlement.

The section concludes with a crucial subject: how to use the foreign exchange markets, be it for spot or forward transactions. This topic will be continued in later sections, especially Section 7.

4.1 SPOT RATES

In the spot market, currencies are bought or sold for immediate delivery, which in practice means settlement in two working days. The exchange rates at which the currencies are bought and sold for immediate delivery are called **spot exchange rates** or **spot rates**. Settlement of a spot currency transaction must be made on the due day, neither earlier nor later. Note that you met the idea of 'spot delivery' in Unit 7; most banking loan and deposits start at 'spot', i.e. the term of the loan or deposit begins two working days after the dealing date.

A foreign exchange rate is the price of one currency in terms of another. Foreign exchange dealers quote two prices: one for buying the foreign currency, one for selling. There are two ways of quoting these rates: the direct quote and the indirect quote. The **direct quote** gives the quotation in terms of the number of units of home currency needed to buy one unit of foreign currency. The **indirect quote** gives the quotation in terms of the number of units of foreign currency bought with one unit of home currency. The following are examples of direct quotes, written as if we were in New York.

GBP1 = USD1.6121

EUR1 = USD0.9055

CHF1 = USD0.7935

Examples of the indirect quote in London are as follows.

GBP1 = USD1.6121

GBP1 = EUR1.4710

GBP1 = CHF2.4084

For discussion of reciprocals, see *Vital Statistics*, Section 1.2.5.

Whether the rate is quoted in the direct or the indirect method, it is easy to find the other way of quotation since one is the reciprocal ($1/x$) of the other. If the quotation is given in the indirect method as GBP1 = USD2, the reciprocal of this is USD1 = GBP0.50 and is a direct quotation. Do not be too concerned about 'direct' or 'indirect', but always know what is being quoted for what. This is easier than it sounds. The following exercise will clarify what is meant.

Activity 4.1

If you asked a foreign exchange dealer for a GBP/EUR quotation and you heard '1.47', what would you think was meant?

From reading the paper or any other general news source, you would know that the rate was about EUR1.5 per pound rather than GBP1.50 per euro. So you would automatically understand what the quoted price meant.

Incidentally, this exercise also shows why reliance on the terms 'direct' and 'indirect' is not always meaningful. Assume that you were in London and were calling a dealer in Frankfurt. Is EUR1.47/GBP1 a direct or an indirect quotation? It is both – or neither. The Frankfurt dealer sees it as direct, you regard it as indirect. But the actual quotation is unaffected by the geographically-based terminology.

The spread between the rates for buying and selling currency represents the dealer's margin, one of the potential sources of profit for the dealer. The size of this spread varies according to the depth of the market (or the volume of transactions), and volatility at the time. A quote from a dealer in London of USD1.6015–1.6025 shows a spread of USD0.0010, ten points. A point is a unit of decimal, the fourth place to the right of the decimal point (0.0001) A pip is the fifth place to the right (0.00001). Most currencies are of a suitable size for one point to be the fourth decimal place. You may find it interesting to look at the spread of rates quoted for retail purchases and sales of foreign currencies at your local bank or currency shop. The spread for a USD/GBP purchase or sale can be 10 cents!

The way the dealer quotes the spot rate and spread for a currency can be confusing, so let us use the *Financial Times* to see how rates are quoted in London (Table 4.1 opposite).

Table 4.1   Spot, forward against the pound

7 August 1998	Currency	Closing mid-point	Change on day	Bid/offer spread	Day's mid High	Day's mid Low	One month Rate	One month % PA	Three months Rate	Three months % PA	One year Rate	One year % PA	Bank of England index
Notes		(1)	(2)	(4)	(3)								
Europe													
Denmark	DKK	11.0337	0.0342	269–405	11.0512	11.0074	11.0018	3.5	10.9378	3.5	10.6961	3.1	106.1
Greece	GRD	479.428	0.404	123–733	481.412	477.38	481.218	-4.5	484.662	-4.4	496.228	-3.5	62.9
Norway	NGK	12.35997	0.0316	526–668	12.4009	12.3206	12.3376	2.1	12.2962	2.1	12.1517	1.7	95.9
Sweden	SEK	13.0682	0.0556	568–795	13.093	13.0248	13.0309	3.4	12.9575	3.4	12.6739	3	84.1
Switzerland	CHF	2.4347	0.0037	333–361	2.4398	2.4308	2.4224	6.1	2.3992	5.8	2.3101	5.1	105.5
Euro	EUR	1.4683	0.0033	675–691	1.4717	1.4665	1.464	3.5	1.4555	3.5	1.4197	3.3	
Americas													
Argentina	Peso	1.6316	-0.0009	312–320	1.6359	1.6313							
Brazil	Real	1.9057	-0.0024	50–63	1.9117	1.9045							
Canada	CAD	2.4817	-0.0069	806–827	2.5097	2.4716	2.4764	2.6	2.4668	2.4	2.4339	1.9	78.1
Mexico	New peso	14.7006	-0.026	6913–7009	14.7767	14.6662	14.8844	-15	15.2796	-15.8	17.1853	-16.9	
USA	USD	1.6324	-0.0004	320–328	1.6362	1.6315	1.6297	2	1.6244	2	1.6049	1.7	114.5
Pacific/Middle East/Africa													
Australia	AUD	2.7168	0.0138	150–186	2.7292	2.6961	2.7109	2.6	2.7	2.5	2.6585	2.1	82.2
Hong Kong	HKD	12.647	-0.0043	439–518	12.6792	16.6341	12.7178	-6.6	12.8049	-5	13.2614	-4.9	

Sterling index calculated by the Bank of England. Base average 1990 = 100 Index rebased 1.12.95. Bid, offer and mid-rates in both this and the dollar Spot tables derived from THE WM REUTERS CLOSING SPOT RATES.

Source: *Financial Times,* 7 August 1998

Some values are rounded by the FT.

All rates are quoted using the indirect method. These rates are taken from representative participants in the London foreign exchange markets at around 16.00 each trading day.

Explanations of terms in Table 4.1

Closing mid-point (1), change on day (2), day's mid (high and low) (3)

These represent the previous day's closing price for immediate, i.e. spot, delivery of GBP, the mid-point between the prices at which they can be bought and sold (1); the change on the previous day's price (2); and the day's high and low for mid-point prices (3).

Bid/offer spread (4)

These are the rates offered by dealers for selling and buying currency. Only the last three decimal places are shown. The foreign exchange dealer in this situation is the **market maker** who is the person posting the rates; the **market user** (yourself) is the person who takes the rates as given. This is true whether the quotation is direct or indirect. Now, if you wanted to go into the market and buy Australian dollars (AUD), for spot delivery, which is the appropriate rate?

First you have to understand that when you, as an organisation, want to *buy* currency, the foreign exchange dealer is then *selling* that currency to you. Therefore you must establish what rate the dealer is quoting as his rate for *selling* AUD. The rate for the dealer selling is AUD 2.7150. This is calculated by taking the closing mid-point for AUD, 2.7168, and changing the last three decimal places (168) to the last three decimal places of the bid price (150). This is quoted in column 4 and is the dealer's selling rate for spot AUD.

The buying and selling rates are shown in Table 4.2.

Sell   Buy.

Table 4.2 Spot rates		
	Bid	**Offer**
Closing mid-point (1)	2.7168	2.7168
Bid/offer spread (4)	150	186
Spot rate	2.7150	2.7186

The dealer could sell us AUD 2.7150 for GBP1 or AUD 2.7186 for GBP1. Using the maxim 'the dealer always wins', the dealer will use the lower bid rate of AUD 2.7150, giving us as few AUD as possible.

The buying and selling rates are quoted together as the **bid–ask spread**.

Activity 4.2 _____

Using the *Financial Times* table, try to see what the rates are if you, as an organisation, want to:

(i)   buy NGK spot   1 235 526
(ii)   buy HKD spot   12.439
(iii) sell EUR spot   .4691
(iv)   sell USD spot.   .6320

Remember that when you sell one currency, you are simultaneously buying another. So when you are *selling* AUD you are also *buying* GBP. So the *bid price* actually refers to buying GBP and the *offer price* is the rate at which the bank will sell GBP. In other words, banks always win and thus, the lower limit of the spread (bid price) is the rate at which the bank will *buy from you*. The upper limit of the spread (offer price) is the rate at which the bank will *sell to you*.

4.2   CROSS RATES

So far we have seen how spot rates are normally quoted. That is fine if we want, for example, a USD/CHF exchange rate, because such rates are quoted explicitly. But what if we needed to sell Swiss francs against New Zealand dollars? We would require a CHF/NZD exchange rate. Normally only USD/CHF and USD/NZD rates are immediately available, so we need to be able to calculate **cross rates** from the set of standard quotations (usually against the USD) that are readily available. The procedure is very straightforward: we compute the required rates *as if* we had bought and sold the 'intermediate' currency. So in our CHF/NZD example, given that we know the CHF/USD and NZD/USD spot rates, we would first 'buy' USD with our CHF (using the CHF/USD rate), and then 'sell' those notional dollars for NZD at the NZD/USD rate.

Let us use some actual figures to see how to do the actual computation, ignoring the bid–ask spread for simplicity:

> Rates: CHF1.4915/USD1, NZD1.9571/USD1
> (from table listing USD spot rates against currencies, *Financial Times*, 7 August 1998)

> Initial amount: CHF2,000,000

Thus, after Stage 1 we would have USD(2,000,000/1.4915) = USD1,340,931.95, and after Stage 2, we would have NZD(1,340,931.95 × 1.9571) = NZD2,624,337.92.

So we have exchanged CHF2,000,000 for NZD2,624,337.92. This gives us an effective NZD/CHF exchange rate of

$$\frac{2,624,337.92}{2,000,000} = 1.3122 \text{ NZD/CHF}$$

Exercise 4.1 _____

If we had required a rate to buy CHF with pounds, how would we have calculated the right rate? Assume CHF1.4915/USD1 and USD1.6324/GBP1.

We can generalise the system to say:

> Multiply or divide the known rates so that the unwanted middle currency can be cancelled out.

In our example we had exchange rates for CHF/USD and NZD/USD so we had to divide the latter by the former to get (NZD/USD)/(CHF/USD) = (NZD/USD) × (USD/CHF) = (NZD/CHF) as required:

$$\frac{\text{NZD/USD}}{\text{CHF/USD}} = \frac{1.9571}{1.4915} = 1.3122 \text{ NZD/CHF}$$

– the same result as we calculated before.

Handwritten notes in right margin:

$USD = \dfrac{2,000,000}{1.4915}$

$NZD = \dfrac{2,000,000}{1.4915 \times 1.9571}$
$=$

1.6324

$CHF \ 2.4347/GBP.$

In the exercise above you had (CHF/USD) and (USD/GBP) so to be able to 'cancel out' the USD you should multiply the rates: (CHF/USD) × (USD/GBP) = (CHF/GBP).

This procedure always works, regardless of whether the rates are spots or forwards. In fact the *Financial Times* quotes cross rates for the major currencies, calculated using this method.

4.3 FORWARD EXCHANGE RATES

A forward exchange agreement is an over-the-counter deal between specific parties and cannot be traded.

A **forward exchange contract** is an agreement to deliver a specified amount of one currency for a specified amount of another currency at some future date. For example if you as a UK company know that you will be receiving USD500,000 in six months' time, your company might well want to know exactly how much GBP they will receive for those USD. It is possible to obtain a quote for a **forward exchange rate** (or **forward rate**) in six months for the USD/GBP and, by booking a six-month forward contract at this rate for the sale of these USD, your company will know now exactly what GBP it will receive in six months' time. Of course, the forward agreement is a binding contract and must be completed on the due date. Otherwise the bank acting as counterpart is entitled to apply a penalty (more on this in sections 4.4 and 8.1). Before we go on to see how forward contract rates are quoted and what determines them, we should look at a few terms that are often heard.

If a currency is trading at a **discount** this means that the currency is weaker in the forward market. If a currency is trading at a **premium** this means that the currency is stronger in the forward market. The impact of this on forward v. spot rates can be shown with an example. If the spot USD/GBP rate is quoted in London as USD1.60 = GBP1, and the forward rate for three months' time is quoted as USD1.64 = GBP1, then we would say that the USD is currently trading at a discount to the GBP, i.e. GBP1 will buy more USD in three months' time than now (and the GBP is trading at a premium to the USD).

Alternatively, if the spot rate for CHF/GBP is 2.45, and the six month forward rate is 2.39, then GBP1 will buy fewer CHF in six months' time, and the CHF is trading at a premium to the GBP. This premium or discount represents the difference between the forward rate and the spot rate for the currencies.

Exercise 4.2

What is the difference between saying 'sterling is trading at a discount with respect to the Swiss franc' and saying 'the Swiss franc is trading at a premium with respect to sterling'?

Forward rates can be quoted in two ways, either as a **forward outright rate** or as a **forward margin**. The former is the complete rate that you would apply to calculate how much of currency X was equal to currency Y in the forward deal. The latter is the difference, measured in points, between the forward outright rate and the spot rate, that is:

Forward outright = Spot + Forward margin

Why make this peculiar division? Because, as we shall see, the forward margin depends primarily on the interest differential between the two currencies; it is therefore more stable than the spot rate (because interest rates move more slowly). As a result, it is more practical to show the volatile part (the spot rate) and the stable part (the forward margin) separately, bearing in mind that banks have to display (through Reuters and other market information systems) continually updated rates.

Remember at the beginning of Section 4 we said that the forward rate was just the spot rate adjusted for a delay in settlement. This 'interest differential' reflects the delay and can be illustrated as follows (ignoring all bid–offer spreads).

Assume that an investor has GBP100,000 which she wants to invest for a year and she can invest in GBP or USD; at the end of the period she wants to end up with USD (perhaps the business has contracted to buy some US asset in one year's time). The current spot rate for USD/GBP is USD1.60 = GBP1. The forward rate for exchanging USD into GBP is USD1.57 = GBP1. Annual interest rates in the USA and the UK for similar risk-free securities are 5% and 7% respectively. The investor has to decide whether she should put her GBP100,000 into USD now and invest in dollars or invest it in the UK and book a forward exchange deal to provide the dollars when required. What should she do?

Exercise 4.3

Before you undertake any calculations, given the interest rates noted here, would you expect the GBP to purchase more USD in one year's time or less?

It is easiest to show the decision for the investor in a diagram (see Figure 4.1).

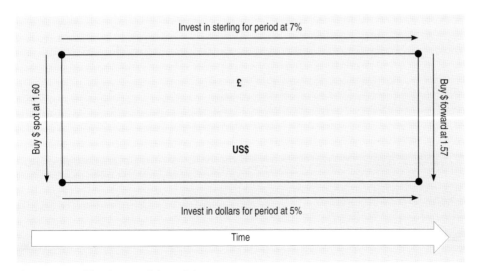

Figure 4.1   The 'rectangle' model

It is very important to realise that all transactions are booked at the start of the deal, whichever 'route' is chosen. Thus the 'buy $ forward' is shown at the end of the rectangle because that is when settlement takes place; however, the rate is 'locked in' right at the beginning of the period, as for the spot rate and the two currencies' interest rates.

As you can see from the above diagram, the investor should be indifferent between investing in USD or in GBP because she is just choosing between alternative routes 'around the rectangle'. Let us work out the numbers and see if they are actually equivalent.

Option 1: Invest in the UK and book forward exchange.

This will involve investing at the sterling interest rate of 7% for one year and exchanging the funds at 1.57, the forward exchange rate. As mentioned before, the forward rate will have been booked at the start of the deal, and it is only settlement which is delayed by one year.

Thus the end result of taking Option 1 would be:

> Investment: £100,000 × 1.07 = £107,000
>
> Exchange: £107,000 × 1.57 = $167,990

Alternatively:

Option 2: Buy USD spot and invest in the USA.

This choice would give figures of:

> Exchange: £100,000 × 1.60 = $160,000
>
> Investment: $160,000 × 1.05 = $168,000

The very small difference of $10 is caused by rounding errors due to only quoting the exchange rates to two decimal places (in practice, rates would usually be specified to four decimal places), and the two routes can legitimately be seen as equal. This is an example of what is known as interest rate parity. The forward rate for GBP against the USD reflects the difference between the interest rate on GBP and the interest rate on USD (strictly their **Eurocurrency** equivalents). If it did not, opportunities for risk-free gains, or arbitrage, would arise; supply and demand would then rapidly ensure that the two routes returned to equivalence.

Interest rate parity is discussed in section 5.1.

Activity 4.3

Work out for yourself what would happen if the interest rates were the same as in the preceding example but a trader quoted the forward rate at the same level as the spot rate. What transactions would you do to make a profit out of the dealer? If lots of people did similar trades with him, what would his overall position look like? How would that make him change his forward rate quotation?

If the investor stays in GBP she will get £107,000 at the end of the year. If she moves into USD immediately and converts back into GBP at the end of the year she will only get £105,000.

To make a profit out of the dealer the investor should borrow USD, convert it into GBP at the 1.60 rate and put the GBP on deposit. The investor should also take out a forward contract to buy USD in one year's time in order to pay off the initial USD loan.

It is important to note that this is a very straightforward way of calculating the forward exchange rate if you are given the spot rate and relevant interest rates. However, for everyday use it is better to encapsulate available information into an equation which can be applied directly and quickly. The formula below is used to calculate the forward margin rather than the forward outright rate itself, for the reason previously discussed about relative stability of exchange and interest rates. Thus the equation for the forward margin (FM) is:

$$FM = \frac{(\text{Period in days}) \times (\text{Spot rate}) \times (i(\text{F}) - i(\text{L}))}{(360 + (\text{Period in days}) \times i(\text{L}))}$$

where $i(F)$ and $i(L)$ mean the interest rate per annum on foreign currency F and local currency L respectively, both written as decimals not percentages (i.e. 0.07 not 7%). Also, the (F) and (L) currencies are connected by the spot rate (S) such that: $F = S \times L$. In other words, the spot rate is defined as the number of units of currency F per unit of currency L (it is very important to get this the right way round).

The figure 360 is a market convention; it is meant to represent the number of days in the year. Box 4.1 explains why.

BOX 4.1   TRADE CALCULATIONS WITHOUT CALCULATORS

Why does the international banking market seem to think that the world goes round the sun once every 360 days rather than the more common notion that it takes about 365.25 days?

This is a continuation of a habit developed by the medieval ancestors of today's bankers. When allowing credit for trade goods, typically evidenced by a bill of exchange, the merchants would usually give the customer 30, 60, 90 or 180 days before payment became due. Before the advent of electronic calculators (or even the older, mechanical sort) to work out the interest payable it was much easier to divide by 360 rather than 365. The typical periods then just reduced to dividing by 12, 6, 4 or 2 corresponding to 30, 60, 90 or 180 days. This practice survives to this day.

It also meant that the actual interest rate being charged was a tiny bit higher, by a factor of 365/360. But your average medieval customer was not highly trained in the devilry of arithmetic – and the merchants weren't going to tell them!

You do not need to be able to prove the formula, just be able to use it and to understand the principle of the 'round the rectangle' arbitrage relationship it comes from. However, for those who are more mathematically inclined and prefer to see the algebra, the formal proof of the formula is shown in the Appendix to this unit.

Let us apply the forward margin equation to our 'round the rectangle' example. If we take GBP as our local (L) currency and USD as our foreign (F) currency, then

$$FM = \frac{360 \times 1.60 \times (0.05 - 0.07)}{(360 + (360 \times 0.07))}$$

$$FM = -0.03$$

The forward outright rate for USD/GBP is therefore:

Forward outright $=$ Spot $+$ FM

Forward outright $= 1.60 - 0.03 = 1.57$ USD/GBP

The forward outright rate of 1.57 is the same as in our original example.

The opportunity for 'risk-free' gains does not arise in real life because, as soon as the rates move out of line, traders arbitrage the gain and reap the benefits themselves, instantly causing the prices to correct themselves before any significant misalignment can occur. In the foreign exchange market itself, dealers will have calculated the forward margin for the forward rate for currency exchange with reference to the difference in interest rates between the two currencies.

Organisations use forward exchange agreements to secure the value of future cash flow(s).

BOX 4.2   FORWARD MARGINS IN THE FINANCIAL TIMES

As dealers give their quotes for forward exchange rates as forward margins, it is useful to show you how to fish them out by interpreting financial newspapers. The key idea is to remember that in the *Financial Times* premiums or discounts are quoted in two different ways: as an absolute amount to be added or subtracted from the spot rate, and as a percentage of the spot price at an annual rate.

Let's look at a more recent example than the numbers in Table 4.1, specifically to the closing mid-point rate of two (soon to disappear) European exchange rates against the British pound at the close of business on March 6 2000:

	Closing mid-point	1 month rate	%pa	3 month rate	%pa	1 year rate	% pa
Belgium	66.3265	66.1804	2.6	65.9093	2.5	64.8186	2.3
Greece	548.585	550.104	−3.3	551.932	−2.4	549.296	−0.1

You can double check for consistency:

	Closing mid-point	(Spot / F) − 1 * (12/period in months) * 100 =	%pa
Belgium	1 month	(66.3265/66.1804) − 1 * (12/1) * 100 =	2.6
Greece	3 month	(548.585/551.932) − 1 * (12/3) * 100 =	−2.4

In brief, to see how the forward margin is accrued you need both local and foreign interest rates; and make use of our 'round the rectangle' approach or the forward margin equation.

Information provided by Hor Chan (B821 Course Tutor) and Peter Warburton (B821 Alumnus).

Eurocurrency is currency traded on the Euromarkets, markets which are free of national restrictions such as witholding taxes or restrictions on interest rates. A Eurocurrency interest rate is the interest rate paid on a Eurocurrency deposit or payable on a Eurocurrency loan. The market is international, with London the major centre.

In practice, forward rates are determined under normal conditions by differences in **Eurocurrency interest rates** – 'Euro-rates'. Thus, the forward rate of GBP against the dollar depends on the difference between the interest rate on **Eurosterling** and the interest rate on **Eurodollars**. Essentially, the Euromarkets are free markets and can be freely used by all major market participants, and thus are the appropriate rates to use. As, we hope, you realised by considering Activity 4.3, unless the **arbitrage condition** held almost exactly, there would be a rapid and heavy movement of funds to profit from the difference. The laws of supply and demand would then cause the interest rates and exchange rates to change in such a way as to eliminate the differential.

Exercise 4.4

Calculate the annual forward margin as a percentage for the earlier 'round the rectangle' example.

4.4 HOW TO USE THE SPOT AND FORWARD EXCHANGE MARKETS

As already said, in a currency deal made for forward delivery, currencies are bought or sold *now* for future delivery. Though the exchange rate is agreed upon today, payment is in the future. This contrasts with a deal done for spot delivery, where the currencies are received and paid in two working days, which is generally thought of as 'now' – after allowing a decorous time interval to allow for all the back-room procedures needed to make settlement happen.

Forex dealers at work

Why two working days? Consider a dealer in Tokyo talking to one in San Francisco. Given time zones and the International Date Line, if it is afternoon of day n in San Francisco, it is already the morning of day $(n + 1)$ in Tokyo. Since both sides really need at least one day to ensure that all processes are completed satisfactorily, the practical minimum interval which should allow all situations to be catered for was decided to be two working days. So 'spot' is typically in two days' time; this does not mean that it is impossible to get 'tom' or 'tod' (tomorrow or today) delivery in many circumstances, e.g. for countries within Europe, but the international standard for delivery is 'spot'. Anything else must be requested specifically.

This discussion about spot can be looked at another way, in order to see once again the link between spot and forward deals. You could regard spot as a 'very short forward', where the delay is a matter of two days rather than weeks or months; again, the point is that spots and forwards are only a time interval apart, they are not inherently different.

As London has, at the time of writing, the biggest foreign exchange market in the world, it is possible to obtain either spot or forward contracts for foreign exchange for almost any currency, for any amount and for most time spans (this last point not applying to spots!). Forex is an **over-the-counter** (OTC) market where there is no central market-place or exchange and each transaction takes place directly between the counterparties concerned. For spot transactions this is an advantage as banks are usually the best sort of institution to effect money transfers on a global basis, and this can be directly encapsulated in the settlement instructions which form a natural part of an OTC deal. This ease of transfer also applies to forwards, but with this latter product there is also a potential disadvantage in that, unlike exchange-traded products, you cannot cancel a trade simply by entering into an equal and opposite deal. As in any OTC market, if you wish to get out of a deal you are either forced to go back to the original counterparty, who will thus know what you wish to do before quoting a price, or to enter into an opposite deal with someone else. In this latter case, both transactions remain 'live' until settlement; this has some administrative and credit implications, but is not usually a major concern – particularly since forward exchange deals are not normally undertaken with an expectation of reversing them before maturity.

Any forward contract involves a certain amount of **credit risk**, since there is always the risk that a party to the contract may default. We will discuss **settlement risk**, which is the risk that on delivery day you pay your side of the bargain but the counterparty fails to pay you, in Section 8 of this unit; here we are concerned about the risk of a counterparty failing during the period between agreeing the deal and maturity. What is at risk if this happens? Not the full amount of the principal since you have not paid anything over to the other side. No, the risk is that you have to replace the deal with the failed counterparty with a new one at rates current at the time of the new deal. Of course, rates may have moved against you, and thus there is a risk. Banks recognise the existence of this form of credit risk and, therefore, if you enter into a forward contract with your bank it will treat as 'used up' a small portion of your borrowing limit until the contract is fulfilled. Typically the amount involved is about 5–15% of the value of the forward exchange deal; it is important to realise that this is not a loan on which you are charged interest, merely a temporary reduction in the total the bank is willing to extend to you as borrowings.

There are no fees, normally, if you take out a forward contract with the bank, which makes its money from the bid–offer spread; you may be charged for the eventual funds transfer, but this would not be a fee for the exchange transaction itself. Of course, the forward deal is a binding contract and must be completed on the due date or the bank acting as counter-party is entitled to levy late payment charges.

BOX 4.3 FORWARDS OF ALL SORTS

As though there aren't enough pressures confronting front-rank football clubs nowadays, they can add foreign exchange risks to the list.

Picking the right player from the cream of overseas clubs is hard enough but, with huge transfer fees, every aspect of a big-name signing is critical. No need to remind Everton, which has just lost out in two dollar-denominated transfer deals because of unhelpful exchange rates.

Mike Cheston, the club's financial controller, tells Foreign Exchange Letter that, from now on, Everton may use 'forwards' – and he's not talking about sending in numbers 9 and 10.

Meanwhile, Manchester United bought the Spanish peseta forward to help pay for Barcelona's Jordi Cruyff. Not only has Cruyff played poorly since, but the peseta has plunged against the pound; it would have been cheaper to buy pesetas at spot prices rather than in advance.

Financial Times, Observer column, 22 January 1997

The advantages and disadvantages of using forward contracts

By entering into a forward foreign exchange contract a UK importer or exporter can:

- fix at the time of the contract a price for the purchase or sale of a fixed amount of foreign currency at a specified future time
- eliminate its exchange risk due to future foreign exchange rate fluctuations
- calculate the exact domestic currency (GBP) value of an international commercial contract despite the fact that payment is to be made in the future in a foreign currency.

A **premium** of the foreign currency shows that the currency is 'stronger' than GBP in the forward market. This means that when entering into a forward contract:

- the UK *exporter* will receive more GBP for the currency export proceeds at the future date than at the spot rate current at the time the contract is taken out

- the UK *importer* will have to pay more GBP to settle its currency debts at the future date than at the spot rate current at the time the contract is taken out.

A **discount** of the foreign currency shows that the currency is 'weaker' than GBP in the forward market. This means that when entering into a forward contract:

- the UK *exporter* will receive fewer GBP for the currency export proceeds at the future date than at the spot rate current at the time the contract is taken out

- the UK *importer* will have to pay fewer GBP to settle its currency debts at the future date at the spot rate current at the time the contract is taken out.

In deciding whether to use the forward market, an organisation will be led by its policy towards risk, but it should in any case make an assessment of what the future spot rate is likely to be. Assume that the company has a one-month forward payment of USD to make, that is, it wants to sell forward GBP. The organisation has three choices: first, it can sell GBP forward now; secondly, it can sell GBP spot for USD, put the USD on deposit for one month (and 'borrow' the GBP needed) and pay out when the deposit matures. The third alternative is to wait for one month and then sell GBP spot.

Exercise 4.5 _____

Are there really three independent alternatives?

_____

The next step is to calculate the forward outright rate.

Assume the rates are as follows (assuming the forwards are in equilibrium with the interest rates): spot: USD1.6060, one-month interest rates: USD: 4%, GBP: 9%. (You may ignore bid–offer spreads.)

Taking the period as 30 days, we can use the 'rectangle diagram' approach we looked at in the preceding sub-section (see Figure 4.2 overleaf).

To clarify the numbers in the diagram, if she invests in sterling for 30 days at 9% per annum, £1 would grow to £1.0075. Similarly, if she invested in dollars at 4%, $1.606 (i.e. £1 × spot rate) would grow to $1.6114. Thus the forward rate will be 1.6114/1.0075 = 1.5994.

If the importer thinks that the spot dollar rate for the pound will actually be USD1.61/GBP1 in a month's time, what should she do?

This decision involves individual judgement, but look at the risks v. the benefits. If the importer's estimate (guess) is correct, and she backs her opinion (by not covering forward) she will have 'won' compared to the safe strategy. But what if the GBP has a bad month? She could lose the company far more. In general, it can be said that she should normally lock in the rate by using the forward market, unless there is a very clear reason for not doing so in particular circumstances. The decision should be determined by the impact the potential losses could have on the organisation, rather than by an

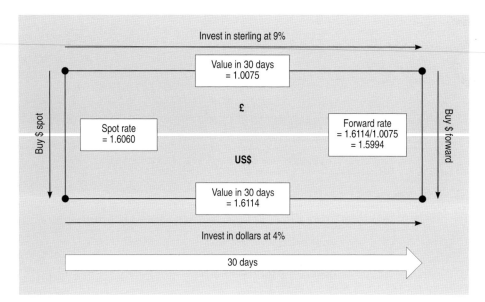

Figure 4.2

individual view of how exchange rates are likely to move. If she chooses not to hedge because she believes the spot rate will be 1.61, she is effectively saying she knows better than the market. Even by doing nothing she is in effect speculating against the market – she would do well to remember that the market comprises a lot of people who make an excellent living by taking bets from corporate treasury departments.

We can see from the above that forward cover can be a cost or a benefit but that the removal of uncertainty – allowing more accurate budgeting – is often of prime importance. Companies operating on high turnover and small profit margins are usually advised to take out forward cover, since the uncertainty involved in not hedging may cause fluctuations in eventual net proceeds which are greater than the firm's overall margin.

To put it another way, considering that currency fluctuations are often of the order of 10–15% a year, an exporting or importing business that trades on gross margins of the same order would be diversifying 50% of its activity (in profit terms) into currency speculation. If the management feels that trading currency is something in which they have expertise, then fine; if, on the other hand, competitive advantage lies elsewhere, it would probably be prudent to have a normal policy of hedging foreign cash flows – but that would not rule out exceptions deemed worthwhile by the management.

SUMMARY

This has been a long section but it has covered a lot of ground, starting with the basic forex market conventions of direct and indirect quotations discussed in the context of the spot market. That was followed by a demonstration of the way to calculate cross rates.

We then moved on to the forward market, discussing the terms 'premium' and 'discount', 'forward outright' and 'forward margin'. This led to a very important result: the forward margin equals the difference in interest rates between the two currencies involved.

The last part of the section introduced you to the forward markets and the pros and cons of taking out a forward contract. We will return at some length to this in later sections, but before we do so we need to consider another important aspect involved with managing exchange exposure: forecasting.

5 FORECASTING FOREIGN EXCHANGE RATES

Once the total foreign exchange exposure is defined, as discussed in Section 2, an organisation can then decide, given the costs of hedging policies and its attitude to risk, the degree to which it should hedge or leave the position open.

Unless the approach of the organisation is to hedge all currency transactions, no matter what, it will have to consider the analysis – the market's and its own – of the expected future movement of exchange rates. An important step in measuring exchange risk is to try to estimate future exchange rate movements accurately. Broadly speaking, two alternatives are open to the organisation; it can either employ in-house personnel whose job it is to forecast future exchange rates, though this is rare except for the very largest companies such as General Motors. Alternatively, the business may use bought-in exchange rate forecasts. These are supplied by the major banks and by specialist forecasting organisations. Whichever is used, it is important to understand some of the major different approaches to forecasting future foreign exchange rates.

There are generally two overall approaches to forecasting exchange rates: fundamental approaches and technical approaches. We will discuss both types in this section. Major examples of the fundamental approach are: the four-way equivalence model, the balance of payments approach and the monetarist approach. An example of the technical approach is the chartist approach.

5.1 FUNDAMENTAL APPROACHES TO FORECASTING EXCHANGE RATES

Four-way equivalence model – or parity conditions

There are four relationships that are thought to underpin international exchange rates: purchasing power parity theory; the Fisher effect; interest rate parity and expectations theory. These four relationships are jointly called the **four-way equivalence model** and are shown in Figure 5.1 overleaf.

See Section 5.7.4 of *Vital Statistics*.

Purchasing power parity (PPP)

Purchasing power parity (PPP) is based on the 'common sense' idea that a product should cost the same wherever it is available in the world, otherwise opportunities for arbitrage will arise; that is, people will try and buy the product in the cheaper market and sell it in the more expensive market to make a profit. Translated into a more general parity theory, this means that the general level of prices, when converted to a common currency, will be the same in each country; price changes due to inflation

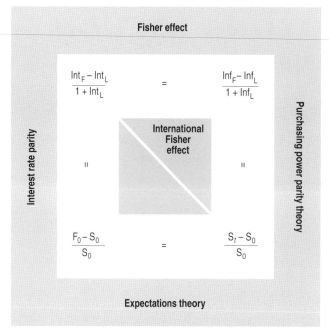

Figure 5.1   The four-way equivalence model

in one country are compensated by a change in the exchange rate so that the real cost of products remains the same. When one country has a higher inflation rate than others, its exchange rate will adjust downwards so that the real cost of products remains the same between countries. Therefore, if the inflation rate in the UK is 8%, and that in the USA is 5% and the spot rate is USD1.5 = GBP1, we would expect the GBP to deteriorate against the USD by, on average, 3% a year. So in a year's time you might expect the exchange rate to have fallen to USD1.455/GBP1.

Though PPP does not hold in the short term, as there are so many market imperfections (taxes, problems of information, quotas), there is evidence to suggest that PPP does hold, on average, in the long term. It therefore should be of interest to those who wish to forecast future exchange rates, as these should move in line with predicted future inflation differentials; this is useful if you need to predict over a long span of time – for example, if you are thinking of building a new factory in a foreign location.

BOX 5.1   PURCHASING POWER PARITY

Assume there are two countries, A and B. The currency of A is the groat (Grt) and a standard loaf of bread costs Grt1; the currency of B is the doubloon (Db), and an identical loaf there costs Db2. In both countries it takes 20 minutes for the average person to earn enough money to buy a loaf.

If the exchange rate at time 0 is Grt1 = Db2, then the 'real' value of the two currencies is the same – the same item (or group of items) costs the same in the two countries. Now assume that there is no inflation in A and 10% inflation of wages and prices in B. At time 7.25 years the loaf should still cost Grt1 in A but now Db4 in B; it still takes 20 minutes' earnings to buy it in either country. If the exchange rate is still locked at Grt1 = Db2, in B all A's goods will be half the price of their (B's) domestic equivalent. A will have an export boom, and all B's bakers – and butchers, candle-stick makers (and manufacturers) – will be

bankrupt and unemployed. To correct the predicament will require deflation in B, which usually means recession. In reality, the government of B would have been forced to act to reduce the inflation rate well before the situation went this far.

Alternatively, if the financial system permitted it, B could devalue its currency with respect to A to restore competitiveness.

If the groat/doubloon exchange rate was free to find its 'natural level' it would change to match the variation in prices in the two countries, so that the same amount of labour continued to earn the same 'real' reward. In this example, the theory says that the exchange rate would stabilise at Grt1 = Db4. The ability to buy goods remains in balance: purchasing power parity.

The Fisher effect

The **Fisher effect** states that the nominal interest rate is made up of two components: a required real rate of return, and an inflation premium equal to the expected rate of inflation. Thus:

$$1 + \text{Nominal rate} = (1 + \text{Real rate})(1 + \text{Expected inflation rate})$$

Vital Statistics, Section 4.4.2, discusses the Fisher effect in greater detail.

As with PPP theory above, the Fisher effect relies on the activities of arbitrageurs, who will move capital from countries with low rates of return to countries with high rates of return. If real rates of interest are thought to be the same worldwide, the difference in nominal interest rates between countries should be due to differences in inflation rates.

The Fisher effect and purchasing power parity together make up the International Fisher effect, which holds that interest rate differentials between countries should be reflected in the expectation of the future spot rate of exchange. PPP states that a rise in the home country's inflation rate will also be accompanied by a **devaluation** of the home country's currency. However, the International Fisher effect states that the increase in inflation means that an increase in the home country's interest rate relative to foreign interest rates will also take place.

The interest rate parity theory (IRP)

The theory of **interest rate parity** (**IRP**) states that the difference in the national interest rates for securities of similar risk and maturity should be equal to the difference between forward and spot rates of exchange (ignoring transaction costs); i.e., the forward premium or discount is equal to the interest differential. The key to this parity condition is the arbitrage relationship you saw in the Section 4 debate about forward rates: if the forward premium or discount is not equal to the interest differential, there are opportunities for risk-free arbitrage. In effect this parity condition means that a country with a lower interest rate than another should value its forward currency at a premium in terms of the other country's currency.

Exercise 5.1

If the annual interest rate in the UK is 13%, that in the USA 10% and the current spot rate between the two countries is USD1.50 = GBP1, assuming interest rate parity holds, what is the forward rate of exchange one year ahead?

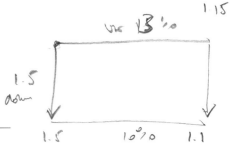

Expectations theory

This is the last parity condition. Central to this relationship is the efficient markets hypothesis (EMH) – that all relevant information should be reflected rapidly and accurately in the market rates. For example, changes in expectations about inflation and interest rates are rapidly incorporated into spot and forward exchange rates. **Expectations theory** also leads to the conclusion that the forward rate of exchange reflects what people expect the future spot rate to be – on average – in the long term. The forward rate is an 'unbiased' estimate of the future spot rate – in the long term. Any changes in expectations are equally likely to cause upward or downward movements of the rates. However, given that this is a long-term average, the forward rate will not always reflect the future spot rate, as shown in Box 5.2 overleaf.

If you would like to refresh your memory on the efficient markets hypothesis, see Unit 1.

The above theory of exchange rate determination is called the four-way equivalence model. The crucial part of this model is that all the parity conditions arrive, eventually, at the same conclusion, namely that the difference between spot and forward rates is just the interest differential between the two currencies. For example, IRP shows it directly as an arbitrage condition, PPP ends up at the same position from the standpoint of long-term economic equivalence of values.

BOX 5.2   ESTIMATION AND PREDICTION IN THE FOUR-WAY EQUIVALENCE MODEL

There is evidence that parts of this model may hold in the long term, but in the short term there may be many market imperfections that mean it does not all hold. Buckley (1996) Chapter 7 gives a good survey of the evidence. Note that IRP does always hold, except for very short periods (i.e. measured in minutes rather than days, before the imbalance is arbitraged away).

So is the forward rate a good estimator of the future spot rate? Yes, in a way. In a statistical sense, it is the 'best estimate' we can achieve, in that it is an unbiased projection of the trend.

Is it a good predictor of the future spot rate? Empirical evidence says, 'No', resoundingly.

How can something be a good estimate but a poor prediction? It is the difference between being right on average and being right on a specific day. Even if the trend in spot rate movement is consistent and follows PPP, the fluctuations around the trend line are so severe – the data are so 'noisy' – that it is seldom much use when trying to predict the actual spot rate for a specific date weeks, months or years in the future. And this is assuming the trend, which itself is based on expected inflation rates (which can change), remains unaltered. Figure 5.2 should give a 'feel' for the problem of 'noisy' data around a trend-line.

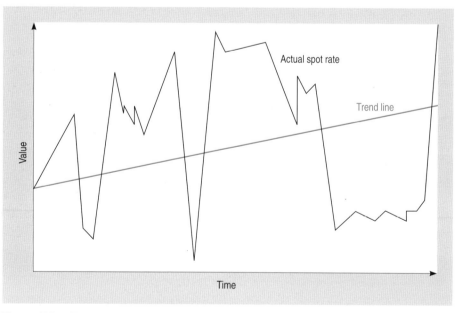

Figure 5.2   Trend with 'noisy' data

To complete this quick review of a somewhat dry economic theory, let us take a look at a very real-world implementation of the PPP concept – with due apology to the vegetarians among our students!

Each year *The Economist* produces its own version of a PPP measure, the Big Mac index. It does this on the grounds that the 'standard loaf of bread' beloved by academics is anything but standard, and so is not very helpful in looking at whether currencies are relatively over- or undervalued. So it looked for another item which was standardised (more or less) around the globe – and found something suitable, namely the Big Mac.

Each Big Mac all over the world is made to the same standard, but using local labour and materials.

Box 5.3 is the text of their 1998 survey.

BOX 5.3   PPP TO GET YOUR TEETH INTO: THE BIG MAC INDEX

As the yen plunges and sterling soars, economists are being forced to revise their currency forecasts. To help them get their teeth into the subject, *The Economist* has updated its Big Mac index, which seeks to make exchange-rate theory a bit more digestible.

The Big Mac index is based upon the theory of purchasing-power parity (PPP), the notion that a dollar should buy the same amount in all countries. Supporters of PPP argue that in the long run, the exchange rate between two currencies should move towards the rate that would equalise the prices of an identical basket of goods and services in each country.

Our 'basket' is a McDonald's Big Mac, produced in 110 countries. The Big Mac PPP is the exchange rate that would leave hamburgers costing the same in America as abroad. Comparing actual rates with PPPs signals whether a currency is under- or overvalued. (For more details on the index, check www.economist.com.)

The first column of the table shows local-currency prices of a Big Mac; the second converts the prices into dollars. The cheapest Big Macs are now in Indonesia and Malaysia, where they cost $1.16.

At the other extreme, Big Mac fans in Switzerland have to pay $3.87. Given that Americans in four cities pay an average of $2.56, the rupiah and the ringgit look massively undervalued, the Swiss franc massively overvalued.

The third column calculates Big Mac PPPs. For example, dividing the Japanese price by the American price gives a dollar PPP of ¥109. On April 6th, the exchange rate was ¥135, implying that the yen is 19% undervalued against the dollar.

Three years ago the index suggested that the yen was 100% overvalued against the dollar. Likewise, the D-mark is now only 5% overvalued, against 50% in April 1995.

Thanks to the dollar's rise – long predicted by burgernomics – it is now closer to its PPP against other big currencies than for many years. Indeed, only five currencies in the table are now significantly overvalued against the greenback, among them Britain's, Sweden's and Denmark's. All three countries have decided not to adopt Europe's single currency, the euro, next year. The pound is 19% overvalued against the dollar, which implies it is 14% overvalued against the D-mark. In contrast, the currencies of the euro-block countries are close to Mcparity against the D-mark.

The most dramatic changes in the index over the past year are in East Asia, where devaluations have left currencies significantly undervalued. This competitive advantage, however, is being eroded by inflation. In Indonesia, the price of a Big Mac has more than doubled over the past year. East European currencies also look cheap, with the Hungarian forint 52% undervalued against the dollar.

The Big Mac index is not a perfect measure of PPP. Price differences may be distorted by trade barriers on beef, sales taxes, local competition and changes in the cost of non-traded inputs such as rents. But, despite its flaws, the Big Mac index produces PPP estimates close to those derived by more sophisticated methods. A currency can deviate from PPP for long periods, but several studies have found that the Big Mac PPP is a useful predictor of future movements – enabling the hungry investor to get rich by putting his money where his mouth is.

Source: The Economist, 11 April, 1998

The hamburger standard

	Big Mac prices		Implied PPP* of the dollar	Actual $ exchange rate 6 April 1998	Under (−) over (+) valuation against dollar %
	local currency	dollars			
United States**	**$2.56**	**2.56**	−	−	−
Argentina	Peso2.50	2.50	0.98	1.00	−2
Australia	A$2.65	1.75	1.04	1.51	−32
Austria	Sch34.0	2.62	13.28	12.96	+2
Belgium	BFr109	2.87	42.58	38.00	+12
Brazil	Real3.10	2.72	1.21	1.14	+6
Britain	£1.84	3.05	1.39***	1.66***	+19
Canada	C$2.79	1.97	1.09	1.42	−23
Chile	Peso1,250	2.75	488	455	+7
China	Yuan9.90	1.20	3.87	8.28	−53
Czech Republic	CKr54.0	1.57	21.1	34.4	−39
Denmark	DKr23.8	3.39	9.28	7.02	+32
France	FFR17.5	2.84	6.84	6.17	+11
Germany	DM4.95	2.69	1.93	1.84	+5
Hong Kong	HK$10.2	1.32	3.98	7.75	−49
Hungary	Forint2.59	1.22	101	213	−52
Indonesia	Rupiah9,900	1.16	3,867	8,500	−55
Israel	Shekel12.50	3.38	4.88	3.70	+32
Italy	Lire4,500	2.47	1,758	1,818	−3
Japan	Yen280	2.08	109	135	−19
Malaysia	M$4.30	1.16	1.68	3.72	−55
Mexico	Peso17.9	2.10	6.99	8.54	−18
Netherlands	Fl5.45	2.63	2.13	2.07	+3
New Zealand	NZ$3.45	1.90	1.35	1.82	−26
Poland	Zloty5.30	1.53	2.07	3.46	−40
Russia	Rouble12,000	2.00	4,688	5,999	−22
Singapore	S$3.00	1.85	1.17	1.62	−28
South Africa	Rand8.00	1.59	3.13	5.04	−38
South Korea	Won2,600	1.76	1,016	1,474	−31
Spain	Pta375	2.40	146	156	−6
Sweden	SKr24.0	3.00	9.38	8.00	+17
Switzerland	SFr5.90	3.87	2.30	1.52	+51
Taiwan	NT$68.0	2.06	26.6	33.0	−20
Thailand	Baht52.0	1.30	20.3	40.0	−49

* Purchasing-power parity: local price divided by price in USA

** Average of New York, Chicago, San Francisco and Atlanta

*** Dollars per pound

Source: McDonald's

Activity 5.1

Log on to the B821 website and access the *Economist* hyperlink. Search in the archive for the most up-to-date article on the Big Mac index; it is updated every year, normally in April.

The balance of payments approach

The **balance of payments approach (BoP)** to forecasting future exchange rates can be best explained by looking at the situation under a system of fixed exchange rates. Box 5.4 explains the simple version of this model, namely that the current account deteriorates when rates of exchange are fixed and the supply of local currency rises. The simple version of this model assumes, when rates of exchange are fixed, that as national income rises, a country's current account deteriorates. The *current account* records trade between countries in actual goods (visible trade) and invisible trade or trade in services, profits from overseas investments, tourism, counsultancy fees, transport-related fees, etc. The domestic currency then tries to weaken, to pay for increased imports, and, within a fixed system, the exchange rate would fall unless the government intervened to counter the effect and correct the current account deficit. In a system of floating rates, when national income rises, the current account deteriorates. The increase in national income leads to increased demand for foreign currency at the expense of home currency. The home currency therefore weakens; exports become more competitive and the current account improves.

The balance of payments is conventionally split into current account and capital account.

In practice even so-called 'fixed' exchange rate regimes normally allow a small band of permissible variation, so the government only has to act when the currency looks like breaching its 'floor' or 'ceiling'.

BOX 5.4   FX AS A PRICE THAT DEPENDS ON SUPPLY AND DEMAND

As you might know, the balance of payments is a summary of all economic transactions between a country and all other countries. Changes in the balance of payments originate in the current account, the capital account or in both the current and capital accounts.

Let us concentrate on how changes in current account modify the balance of payment and this, in turn, foreign exchange. If the current account worsens that means the country's imports are growing at a greater rate than that of exports of goods and services. As the current account worsens, under a fixed exchange rate regime, there will be an increased demand for foreign currency to pay for imports and pressure will mount for the foreign currency to strengthen. The exchange rate will eventually adjust but by discrete changes, usually resulting from a bureaucrat's decision. Notice that an equivalent situation is to increase the supply of the domestic currency, say because of inflation or because people have more to spend (i.e. national income rises thanks to productivity gains).

In a floating exchange rate regime, if imports are growing at a greater rate than exports then the foreign currency will also strengthen but exchange rate will adjust almost immediately. Operations in open markets will record imbalances between imports and exports as they take place. The downside of a floating rate regime, however, is that exchange rates could be more volatile and particularly susceptible to short term variations in the terms of trade; whereas the productivity of a country changes in the medium to long term.

The challenge to forecasting exchange rates using the balance of payments is that proposed adjustments to currency rates are more pervasive: because the bigger the economy, the longer it will take to observe significant changes in the current or capital accounts.

With contributions from Hor Chan, B821 Associate Lecturer.

Modern adherents of the BoP approach to forecasting future exchange rates also look at movements in a country's *capital account*. The capital account details international movements of financial assets and liabilities, e.g. overseas direct investment by a multinational; investments from overseas in local bond and stock markets (sometimes called 'hot money'); and loans from international banks and foreign multinationals to local companies. The capital account does not consider, however, profits or dividends paid by foreign companies to local companies or individuals.

An example of how you must consider both current and capital accounts when looking at balance of payments data to forecast future exchange rates is the USA between 1981 and 1985. During that period the USA had a large and deteriorating current account position. However, the factors promoting investment demand for dollars through the capital account were so strong that the flows necessary to finance the current account deficit were easily forthcoming. Only when the factors promoting capital flows started to move against the dollar (interest rate differentials narrowed, banking problems limited the willingness to hold dollar deposits, and so on) did the current account stand out as a 'problem' as far as the dollar was concerned.

Monetarist approach

Since monetary policy is an attempt to control the supply of **money** to the economy, the **monetarist approach** must be concerned with interest rates – the 'price' of money. But we have seen that interest rates affect exchange rates by both altering the attractiveness of holding a currency as an income generator and by impacting on sentiment about the currency's future prospects. Furthermore, monetarist theory says that too much money chasing too few goods in an economy is a prime cause of inflation – the available cash will increase demand but supply will not increase accordingly, so prices rise and/or imports increase. Thus, an economy with a relatively high money supply growth will experience a weakening exchange rate. This is why exchange dealers and forecasters spend a lot of time analysing (and agonising over) money supply figures.

5.2 TECHNICAL ANALYSIS

Technical analysis refers to the study of the action of the market, especially market prices, as opposed to the study of the companies, countries or goods in which the market deals. **Chartist analysis** is a version of technical analysis which studies market movements exclusively through the use of charts. The technical or chartist analyst does not believe that fundamentals are necessarily unimportant, but believes that there are other influences, perhaps psychological and/or emotional, which are more important.

Technical analysis is an extreme approach based on the idea that past price behaviour will be useful to forecast future values.

All these factors come together in the market-place, primarily, in only one piece of information – the price of the currency, equity or bond. The basic tools for the technical analyst are price charts – time series graphs of prices. For the foreign exchange markets, these charts record, in one form or another, the value of the currency. Readings are typically recorded each day, usually taking closing levels. Over long periods, certain price patterns emerge which are then associated with certain subsequent price developments, so that the subsequent price developments are said to be predictable. Technicians would never claim that such predictability is infallible, but they do aver that certain patterns repeat themselves with sufficient frequency for them to be regarded as highly probable.

Proponents of technical analysis claim it has two great strengths over more fundamental techniques of forecasting exchange rates. First, trends indicated by graphic analysis tend to remove the 'noise' of random movements. So the exchange rate itself is already telling you what all the factors affecting exchange rates are saying. Secondly, at any one moment, the most probable (though by no means certain) next event is a continuation of the past trend. As technicians say, 'the trend is your friend', so stay with it until it changes.

Others would say that technical analysis suffers from mistakenly identifying patterns that are not there, failed genuine patterns, ambiguous patterns and the inability to specify the time period in which targets will be hit. In addition, if the volatility of the market changes, sticking to rigid filter rules will inevitably lead to poor decision-making.

5.3   HOW GOOD IS EXCHANGE RATE FORECASTING?

But is all this prediction of the future from the past valid? At the beginning of this course, in Unit 1, you looked at EMH. Even the weak form of EMH seems to show that future price movements are random and, if this is so, is it not evidence for the fallibility of predicting future trends? However, one of the key assumptions of EMH (rational – and thus profit maximising – behaviour by participants) does not hold at certain times in foreign exchange markets, for example when governments support particular currencies.

In addition, many participants in the foreign exchange market use technical analysis to forecast future exchange rates, so we cannot just ignore it as an inconvenient anomaly. We need to investigate a little of the evidence for and against the benefits of technical analysis.

Activity 5.2 _____

Read the short article posted on the course website, 'Chart analysis and the foreign exchange market' from the *Bank of England Quarterly Bulletin.*

Exercise 5.2 _____

Do the graphs in Chart 3 (in the reading in Activity 5.2) show that the chartists were good forecasters over the period assessed? Is there an irreconcilable conflict between the EMH and the evidence given about technical analysis in the London forex market?

The article should have given you a flavour of what goes on in the dealing rooms of the City of London. As the answers to the questions posed in Exercise 5.2 indicate, the difference in time horizon between a trader for whom (at 7.30 am) lunch-time is the long term and a corporate treasurer concerned about what will happen over the next five years, technical analysis and EMH may not coincide in this specific instance. It is worth noting that most academic studies aiming to test the EMH use data such as daily closing rates – a timescale of the order of a day. The evidence is strong that the hypothesis is true for that sort of horizon – but that does not prove or disprove the validity of chartism when used by practitioners to predict the tiny minute-by-minute reactions of a market that is essentially psychological on that sort of timescale.

It is worth reading or listening to some of the analyses produced by forecasters who claim to be basing their results on technical analysis. If

you dissect carefully what they say, it often contains a lot of economic analysis – that is, fundamental rather than technical. It will usually be very good economic analysis, and the forecasts produced may be very useful, but it is not technical analysis, so do not confuse the two.

In an interview (Kern, 1996), the NatWest team of economists responsible for forecasting movements in exchange rates discussed how they arrived at their forecasts. They commented that chartism was not a big part of the bank's foreign exchange forecasting, although they respected the theory and followed what chartists were saying, 'It is something you have to take into account, because there is a body of market opinion that swears by it.'

5.4 CURRENCY HISTOGRAMS

Once an organisation has reviewed publicly available or in-house forecasts, it can then integrate these forecasts into an analysis of the impact of the movements in the exchange rates on its value.

One means of combining differing estimates of exchange rate movements, as recommended in various textbooks (e.g. Shapiro, 1992), is by the use of **currency histograms**. In this way the exchange rate forecasts from different experts may be weighted by their perceived reliability. This is demonstrated in Figure 5.3 overleaf.

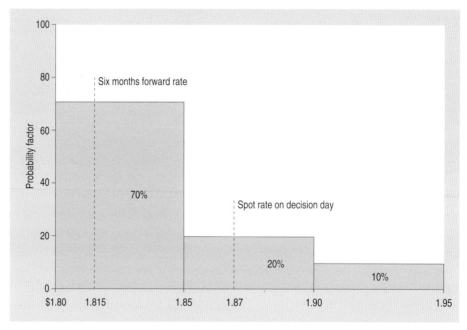

Figure 5.3   A currency histogram

Example

Assume that a number of foreign exchange advisers have been surveyed, and that their views are summarised in Figure 5.3.

70% believe the rate in 6 months' time will be between USD1.80 and USD1.85, 20% between USD1.85 and USD1.90, and 10% between USD1.90 and USD1.95.

Assume also that a UK company has an import duty payable of USD500,000 which is due in six months. On the day on which it must decide on a hedge strategy, the exchange rate for six months forward is USD1.8150 and the spot rate is USD1.8700.

What should the company do? From the histogram it can be seen that there is a very high probability that the rate will be around USD 1.8000–1.8500. Given the company wishes to purchase USD for use in six months' time, then the company would benefit from buying USD through the spot market now since, according to the histogram, there is a good chance that the dollar will have strengthened in six months' time. Another possibility – and probably a more realistic one as the company may well not have the cash available to buy spot – would be to buy dollars forward. As you know, this is equivalent to buying at today's spot rate, with the forward margin merely reflecting the interest differential for the delay in settlement.

Strictly speaking, the histogram does not show that 'there is a very high probability' that the rate will be around USD1.80–1.85. It shows that 'in the opinion of those surveyed, there is a …'; in other words, the information is only as good as those from whom it is obtained and is not absolute. This does not prevent you from using it – a manager always makes the best use of what he or she has to hand – but it is important to include an estimation of the quality of information in your deliberation.

Having reviewed the various forecasts of future exchange rates, the organisation has to decide, on the basis of these forecasts, what action to take with regard to hedging. This decision will also be a function of the organisation's objectives and attitude to risk, which is the main subject of the next section.

SUMMARY

This section has looked at various methods used for trying to forecast exchange rate movements. The approach in Section 5.1 was to apply aspects of economic theory to the problem. The first technique used a number of ideas combined into what is called the four-way equivalence model. This consisted of purchasing power parity, Fisher effect, interest rate parity and expectations theory; they all combined to produce a significant result, that the difference between spot and forward rates was solely due to the interest differential between the currencies, and that the forward rate was an unbiased estimate for the future spot rate. Unfortunately it is unlikely to be a good predictor, but you cannot have everything!

Two other economic viewpoints were introduced, namely the balance of payments and the monetarist approaches, but both of these really analyse the broad sweep of an economy and, while they can be used for considering general trends, are not typically much use at forecasting short-term exchange rates.

The second sub-section discussed technical analysis, a topic which is regarded with deep suspicion by academics – it offends EMH ideas for a start – but one that is used quite a lot in the financial markets. We saw that, while it may have some validity in the extremely short-term outlook of forex dealers, it is very suspect as a tool to use for the time horizons typically needed for conducting 'normal' business.

In Section 5.3 we reviewed the implications of the efficient markets hypothesis for exchange rate forecasting and saw that there are reasons why EMH may not always apply in the foreign exchange markets.

The last topic, discussed in Section 5.4, looked at one way of making use of exchange rate forecasts and currency histograms, realising all the while that they are never more than educated guesses.

The impression may have been given that forecasting exchange rates was rather a pointless activity, given the empirical evidence for its marked lack of success. This may be a reasonable viewpoint when thinking about relatively near-term and quantifiable exposures, e.g. most transaction exposure, because there are good methods available for negating such risk – booking forward as an example. However, when thinking about the broader aspects of, say, economic exposure, it becomes less realistic to expect the organisation to be able to hedge away its risk. Forecasting then becomes an important tool, however good or bad it may be, as a provider of information for managing such exposure. Even if forecasting cannot dictate what to do, it is still an indispensable tool in a range of planning and monitoring functions.

6 FOREX RISK MANAGEMENT WITHIN THE ORGANISATION

An organisation's foreign exchange hedging strategy depends on its objectives and its attitude towards currency risk. Some examples will make this clear:

- a strongly risk-averse manager typically will ensure that any overseas subsidiaries are financed in local currency to minimise translation exposure and that any transaction exposure is fully hedged

- a less risk-averse manager concentrates on economic and transaction risks to some extent; he may ensure a gross match of foreign assets and liabilities to reduce some translation exposure, but with transaction exposure the idea is that, to some extent, he is willing to accept a loss on exchange to keep open the possibility for a gain

- with asymmetrical risk aversion, losses loom larger than gains in the manager's eyes; interest 'costs' are preferable to exchange 'losses'; above a certain trigger level, transaction exposure will usually be hedged

- the aggressive speculator uses the foreign exchange market as just one more potential source of profit.

The idea of being risk-averse was introduced in Unit 1.

The management needs to determine where the organisation stands in its attitude to risk and issue clear and consistent guidance. For example, the stance taken in the 'less risk-averse' case above usually arises from a company view that, on average, gains and losses even out, and thus too much effort taken on hedging is effort wasted.

BOX 6.1   AVERSION THERAPY

In the early 1990s, the author was interviewing the management of a UK company with a turnover of GBP40 million about its hedging policies to foreign exchange exposure. The company had been owner-managed until very recently, and had used a wide range of hedging techniques (options and forwards) as well as deciding in some circumstances, given forecast currency movements, not to hedge. Since the company had been taken over by a large multinational enterprise, its local management had had to follow very strict head office instructions about the hedging of foreign currency exposure. These had included the requirement that they always had to hedge transaction exposure, that they always had to use forward contracts and that these contracts could only be taken out once the amount of the actual transaction exposure was known (e.g. the purchase invoice in foreign currency had been received).

Options are discussed in Unit 9.

This is an example of a very 'risk-averse' approach by head office to currency management.

Activity 6.1 _____

In Box 6.1 you saw two attitudes towards forex risk, one that could perhaps be described as strongly risk-averse and the other as less risk-averse. Think about the attitude in your own organisation. What would you say was the stance of most managers? Are their actions consistent with this view? Are they consistent with stated organisational policy? Indeed, is it clear what is the organisation's policy regarding forex risk?

6.1   THE ORGANISATION OF EXPOSURE MANAGEMENT

Having decided on its overall approach to risk, a multi-divisional organisation will have to decide whether to concentrate all foreign currency management within a centralised treasury function, or to decentralise. Both have their advantages and disadvantages, and in practice most large organisations will operate a mixture. For example, all funding decisions (currency, interest rate, amount) might be taken within a central treasury, but local management will have some discretion over the currency of invoicing. All parts of the organisation, no matter how large or small, should be made aware of the implications for the organisation of currency movements.

Exposure management is needed because the organisation's normal operation is a matter for the purchasing, production and marketing departments, working in conjunction with and drawing on the expertise of the finance department. It necessarily focuses on the change in the value of net cash flows due to unanticipated exchange rate movements. The different departments have different responsibilities, within the overall context of operational exposure management.

The marketing department decides whether to price and invoice in terms of the firm's base currency, or in suitable foreign currencies – thereby potentially taking on foreign currency risk.

The purchasing department decides whether to contract and buy in terms of the firm's base currency, or in suitable foreign currencies – thereby taking on foreign currency risk, depending to an extent on the sales pricing policy.

The production department decides in which countries products should be manufactured. Unsurprisingly, this can have forex risk implications.

The finance or treasury department decides, given other departments' decisions, in which currency to source the necessary funds, how to make that capital available to the relevant areas, and how to implement the exchange exposure policy of the organisation – balancing the needs of the departments against the costs and risk levels considered acceptable.

This might still leave local management with the need to make decisions about whether it should hedge any of its immediate net transaction exposure, given any available forecasts of foreign exchange movements, either from external sources or the finance or economics/planning departments. Clearly, not all organisations will be large enough to warrant – or want – an economics or planning department, say, so local management may well have to rely on its own resourcefulness in order to obtain the best information it can – but it will have to decide in the end.

What matters is not whether rates are going to move against the organisation compared with the spot, but how they will end up compared with the forward. The choice is between the forward rate (achieved through hedging) and the forecast (the best estimate of the future rate without hedging). So does this mean that hedging should be undertaken when the forecast rate is less favourable than the forward rate? Well, yes if the forecast is believed to be reliable. But forecasts can only be more reliable than forward rates if the forex market is inefficient and the expectations theory (see Figure 5.1) fails to hold. While such a belief is not indefensible, it should not be followed too lightly. A sensible *modus operandi* might be to hedge unless there is a good reason not to.

A formal template that might be used, if management believes its forecasts are more reliable than the forward rate, is shown in Table 6.1.

Table 6.1 Using forecasts	Direct quotation		Indirect quotation	
Rate forecast less than forward rate				
Current position:	Net +	Net −	Net +	Net −
Recommended action	Cover forward	Leave open	Leave open	Cover forward
Rate forecast greater than forward rate				
Current position	Net +	Net −	Net +	Net −
Recommended action	Leave open	Cover forward	Cover forward	Leave open
Rate forecast equal to forward rate				
Current position	Net +	Net −	Net +	Net −
Recommended action	Cover forward	Cover forward	Cover forward	Cover forward

'Net +' means a positive net exposure in terms of the relevant foreign currency, 'Net −' a negative net exposure.

Example

Consider the position of a UK company which is dealing with US customers. It is due to receive $100,000 in three months' time. The three-month forward rate is GBP0.6250 = USD1 (direct) or GBP1 = USD1.60 (indirect).

Direct and indirect quotes were discussed in Section 4.1.

The company has a reliable forecast of the three-month forward rate as GBP0.6135 = USD1 (direct) or GBP1 = USD1.63 (indirect).

If it uses a forward it will receive

Direct = $100,000 × 0.625 = £62,500

Indirect = $100,000/1.60 = £62,500

If it chooses not to cover and trades on the spot market in three months' time, the forecast is that it will receive

Direct = $100,000 × 0.6135 = £61,350

Indirect = $100,000/1.63 = £61,350

When performing calculations using foreign exchange rates it is important to work to as many decimal places as possible to avoid rounding errors.

The company would be best advised to cover forward.

Using Table 6.1 to reach the same answer, we have a direct quote, where the forecast rate is less than the forward rate, and a net + cash inflow of the foreign currency, in this case USD. Table 6.1 therefore recommends us to cover forward in line with our manual calculations.

Exercise 6.1 _____

Why is the recommended action always to cover forward (hedge) if the forecast equals the forward rate?

_____

In terms of risk/return, the table's recommendations would mean including a caveat that 'Leave open' should be applied only where the expected extra return justified the extra exchange risk being taken. In other words, 'Leave open' should only be used if the prediction is of a sufficiently high gain, not just of a gain.

6.2   DESCRIPTION OF MANAGEMENT TECHNIQUES

The choice of currency hedging techniques by management is determined by the attitude of the organisation making the choice, but this attitude may well be influenced by the type of the business. A company producing goods for export in foreign currency with imports payable in foreign currency is one type (transaction exposure would be its main concern); a multinational company with extensive international involvement is another (economic exposure may well be the largest component in such a case). The range of techniques open to the latter is typically greater than to the former, simply because scale often means that more methods can be used cost-effectively.

This attitude is also determined by the structure of the organisation and by corporate policy towards exchange risk, which, in turn, is constrained by hedging costs, regulatory constraints, tax effects, and so on. You have already met some of the different types of organisation and their possible different transaction exposures in Section 2. Before we discuss the hedging techniques they could use, it is worth questioning whether the costs of hedging are worth the benefits.

Arguments for not hedging

Some organisations do not hedge their foreign currency flows, taking a 'swings and roundabouts' approach. The concept is that there is no need to manage individual exposures because the overall gains and losses due to currency movements tend to cancel out when everything is consolidated. The assumption is that the activities of the companies involved are so large, varied and evenly spread across currencies that all the individual plus ('long') and minus ('short') positions approximately cancel out.

This requirement is only really fulfilled at the group level of large multinationals, but may be close enough to the truth for smaller organisations to believe that it is not cost-effective to manage the exchange exposure more actively. It does involve a close examination of the organisation's economic exposure and an understanding of the currency trading blocs that operate around the world. An example is trading in Central and Eastern Europe. Many of the emerging economies of Central Europe, e.g. Poland and the Czech Republic, though they have their own currencies, originally pegged their exchange rates closely to the DEM, as Germany is often their largest trading partner. Since the euro is now Germany's currency, it has replaced the Deutschmark as the 'peg' for the Polish zloty or Czech koruna. Thus currency exposure to movements in the Polish or Czech currencies is now linked to movements in the EUR exchange rate.

For a UK business, outside the euro bloc, this change may make little practical difference; similarly for a German company dealing with Poland or the Czech Republic. In the first instance, the zloty or koruna is still pegged to a foreign currency, in the second case it is still pegged to the company's local currency. But for a Spanish or Italian organisation, the difference could be important. The Czech and Polish currency used to be pegged to a foreign currency (the Deutschmark) but now it is linked to the Spanish or Italian local currency – the euro.

Lastly, if it is group-level policy to apply exposure netting across subsidiaries it is important that the separate operating units are then given due allowance for the variability such a policy will cause in their individual profit performances.

Exposure netting means netting off same currency cash flows across operating units to minimise exchange risk in those currencies. It is dealt with in detail in Section 7.1.

'Swings and roundabouts' is an approach which assumes that, on average, hedging is a loss-making activity – even if only to the extent that the bank collects a spread on the purchase or sale – so it is better not to hedge if you can afford not to. That means dealing with unacceptable risks (perhaps by hedging certain major transactions) and not hedging those transactions which, after netting, leave a level of risk that is acceptable.

At the other end of the scale, for very small organisations with limited foreign exchange exposure, management may consider it is not worth hedging given the need to have the relevant monitoring and information systems. There is anecdotal evidence to suggest that many small UK companies, if involved in overseas purchases or sales, get round the problem of currency exposure by ensuring that all invoicing is in GBP.

Exercise 6.2

Why might this not be an appropriate way of dealing with currency exposure?

SUMMARY

In this section we considered how an organisation's approach to risk has an influence on its approach to hedging foreign exchange exposure. We then considered briefly the responsibility of various parts of an organisation when dealing with exchange matters. In essence, departments such as marketing, production and purchasing should take note of the risks of exchange exposure when making their decisions – that is, consider the risk/return trade-off inherent in involving foreign currencies in their operations.

The treasury or finance department should monitor and implement the corporate exchange risk policy, including the procurement of capital with a suitable currency mix. In practice, the implementation role ensures that the treasury department is likely to be involved in the overall foreign exchange determination process of the other departments even if final decisions and actions are taken by them.

Lastly, we considered one argument against hedging foreign exchange exposure, together with a possible rebuttal: in general, policy cannot be prescribed but must flow from the needs and risk-profile of the individual organisation. We will return to this aspect towards the end of Unit 9.

In the next section we move on to look at some of the different techniques for hedging currency exposure.

7 TECHNIQUES FOR EXPOSURE MANAGEMENT

Section 2 outlined the distinctions between exposure. In this section the various techniques available to an organisation for reduction of foreign exchange exposure, be it transaction, translation or economic, are examined.

The range of systems and financial instruments for hedging foreign exchange exposure can be thought of as being plotted along an 'internal–external' axis. Internal describes those methods that involve activities within an organisation to alter the composition of the exposed position. Some of these may even involve reorganisation of the company structure. External covers those techniques which involve the use of outside institutional services and financial markets. So setting off EUR receipts against EUR payments would be internal, but selling EUR forward to a bank for GBP would be external. Later in the section we shall come across other methods that plot somewhere in between.

It is good practice first to use as many internal techniques as possible before resorting to external ones, because on the whole the former work out cheaper overall and may on occasion even prove more efficient. We will follow this 'internal to external' order in our description of the techniques. Bear in mind that all exposure minimisation techniques involve costs of one sort or another and, clearly, only if the benefits outweigh the costs will the techniques be worthwhile.

The main techniques we will cover are listed in Table 7.1.

Table 7.1 Possible foreign exchange risk reduction techniques	
Internal	**External**
Exposure netting	Exchange risk guarantees
Matching	Long-term borrowing in overseas currencies
Pricing adjustments	Financial products (e.g. spots, forwards, futures, options)

This list is by no means exclusive. There are many other different methods of hedging exposure, but these six techniques cover some of the more obvious approaches. Some financial instruments (i.e. options) mentioned in Table 7.1 will be covered in Unit 9; but they are included in this list for completeness.

7.1   TECHNIQUES TOWARDS THE 'INTERNAL' END OF THE SCALE

Technique 1 Exposure netting

Bilateral or multilateral **exposure netting** involves companies in the same group which trade with each other. In bilateral netting, the two associated companies net off the currency amounts that they owe to each other. An example would be where a Hong Kong subsidiary owes a German subsidiary of the same group the HKD equivalent of USD3 million and at the same time the German subsidiary owes the Hong Kong subsidiary the EUR equivalent of USD4 million. The actual remittance to clear the inter-company accounts would be netted to the equivalent of USD1 million to be paid to the Hong Kong subsidiary. In this way the two subsidiaries have saved on transfer and exchange costs.

With multilateral netting, a central treasury function is usually involved. An example would be as follows. In a group of companies, a French subsidiary buys (during the monthly netting period) USD3 million worth of goods and services from a German subsidiary and the French subsidiary sells USD1 million worth of goods to the UK subsidiary. During the same month, the German subsidiary buys USD1 million worth of goods from the UK subsidiary. Settlement of the intercompany debt within the three subsidiaries means a payment equivalent to USD2 million from the French subsidiary to the German subsidiary.

Multilateral netting can bring large savings in exchange and transfer costs, but it requires a centralised communications system. Exchange controls may also put restrictions on these approaches to netting.

Technique 2 Matching

Consider an organisation's assets and liabilities, grouped by currency, as amounts in the pans of a group of balance scales (one per currency). If you add up all the asset amounts and all the liability amounts, the overall total must be equal. But the individual scales need not be in balance – for example, the firm might be financing a Czech factory (koruna assets) with a USD loan (dollar liability). **Matching** may involve rearranging the balance sheet to try to keep each scale individually in balance as much as possible. In other words, to reduce the translation exposure before the event rather than deal with it after the event.

In practice, you have to use mostly external methods (for example foreign currency borrowing) to 'match' long-term assets with long-term liabilities, so we will consider those later in this section. On the other hand, internal methods can often be applied to current cash inflows and outflows with good effect, simply because they are more amenable to influence by managers in the short run. Receipts in a particular currency are used to make payments in that currency, thereby reducing the need for a group of companies to go through the foreign exchange markets.

The way in which matching is run in a large organisation is similar to netting. It usually involves a group treasury, and centralised information of all third-party currency receipts and payments.

The group or central treasury then buys or sells externally any balance of 'un-netted' currency. In this system the central treasury acts, effectively, as banker to all the other units. As soon as an office has a receipt or must pay a foreign currency it sells it to or buys it from the treasury; if one department receives, say, USD and another unit needs to pay out USD, the 'internal banker' method will automatically net out as much as possible. Note that this works for all foreign flows, whether they originate in another part of the same organisation or externally. As long as everyone only deals with the central treasury, netting is automatic. However, this system may only be cost-effective for large organisations able to justify running, in effect, a mini-bank. In addition, for units half-way around the world from the central treasury, not being allowed to deal locally can be an irritant or even a genuine problem.

You will see an example of this 'internal bank' idea when in Unit 9 you study the video case study on TNT International, a major courier company based in the Netherlands.

Technique 3 Pricing adjustments

Let us illustrate this with an example of a pricing policy in need of reassessment. The situation at present is shown below in Table 7.2. With receivables in a currency which devalues and payables in a currency which revalues, the exporter loses. In this case we are being wise after the event, but what could have been done at the start to avoid this problem?

Table 7.2 Exports invoiced in GBP, imports in USD, GBP devaluation			
	Due to receive	Due to pay	Gain/loss
Month 1: GBP = USD 1.6	GBP10,000	USD16,000 = GBP10,000	Nil
Month 2: GBP = USD 1.4	GBP10,000	USD16,000 = GBP11,429	–GBP1,429

Even though the sales and purchases were on budget, a loss was caused in month 2 because of the fall in GBP over the period. What are the company's alternatives?

- It could increase its sales price, but that might make it uncompetitive.
- It could hedge by purchasing dollars forward, but that would lock it into buying USD16,000 regardless of how much stock it found it needed. Also, that would only provide a hedge for the length of time of the forward purchase, i.e. for as long as the exporter felt confident in predicting the required level of payables.
- It could set its sales price in dollars.
- It could ask to be invoiced in GBP.
- It could both set its sales price and be invoiced in a third currency.

All of the last three would ensure that sales and purchases were inherently off-setting, and so automatically hedged each other to the extent that they matched. For example, there would normally be a profit margin which would remain exposed after netting the sales receivables and the purchase payables.

Apart from the profit element, the company would be hedged whatever currency was chosen, provided it was the same for both sales and purchases; given this, the decision as to which currency to use would normally be influenced at least as much by marketing concerns as by risk-reduction ones. However, in some companies, there may be little choice about which currency to use, as the companies may operate in industries which are strongly influenced by one currency. For example, the production and development of aluminium is a USD denominated industry, with aluminium prices denominated in USD everywhere in the world.

Exercise 7.1 _____

How could the company ensure that the profit was also inherently hedged?

_____

The price rise option, number one in the list, is probably only available in two main scenarios – either the company's sales are not price-sensitive or all competitors are subject to the same exchange rate pressure. An example of the latter would be the oil industry and the price of petrol; an example of the former is noted in Box 7.1.

BOX 7.1   AVOIDING FINANCIAL DISCORD

An organisation provided very specialised, tailor made, tour packages for orchestras and other specialist groups who wished to tour abroad (abroad here meant outside the groups' home country). The organisation dealt with all aspects of travel (including the conveyance of musical instruments), accommodation and hire of local halls. As this was a very specialist service, and there were very few competitors, the organisation was able to price its services in GBP.

Inter-company or inter-subsidiary sales is often an area that allows considerable leeway in price-setting. **Transfer pricing**, the choice of pricing of goods transferred between subsidiaries of an organisation, can operate to the organisation's advantage, since it is relatively easy to set fairly arbitrary prices for intra-company transfers of goods and services, as long as you do not go to extremes. The volatility of exchange rates often gives considerable room for manoeuvre: when the usual goal is to maximise profit in the company operating under the lower tax regime, a suitable choice of exchange rate can be very helpful. Tax laws are often designed to prevent excessive manipulation of exchange rates, but if an exchange rate fluctuates by 10% over the life of an intra-company sales contract it is usually possible to justify using a 'suitable' rate! The degree of subjectivity involved means management's choice of a 'fair' price can often lie between rather broad limits.

Transfer pricing can help to eliminate exchange losses in areas of the world where continual devaluations take place, and can involve exchange gains where continual revaluations occur. Often countries with chronic inflation or balance of payments difficulties may limit capital outflows by various means. Transfer pricing may provide the only means for the investor to repatriate earnings from an economy experiencing devaluation and capital outflow controls. Intra-company transfers of goods and services to the subsidiary in question may be marked up in price; alternatively, its exports to affiliated companies may be priced as low as possible. As mentioned in the preceding paragraph, groups operating in several countries ideally make high profits in strong currency, low tax areas; on the other hand, if, as a result of the transfer pricing, earnings were increased in a country with a higher tax rate, this might well be more advantageous than having profits blocked or eroded by a continual depreciation of the local currency.

Transfer pricing does, however, incur costs. It is expensive to administer and it may cause the company to run foul of the tax and customs authorities at home and overseas.

7.2 TECHNIQUES CLOSER TO THE 'EXTERNAL' END OF THE SCALE

Remember, as with 'internal' techniques, 'external' alternatives involve costs (often in terms of profits forgone) and the organisation must ensure that the benefits outweigh the costs before committing itself to one particular technique.

Technique 4 Exchange risk guarantees

Most governments are willing to give some type of guarantee for certain types of exchange risks. Governments, perceiving the benefits of exporting, will normally assist the exporters in many ways, including the provision of **exchange risk guarantees**. These guarantees are often for protecting officially sponsored overseas borrowing. Examples might be socially or economically favoured projects with very long 'lead' times or in countries with no forward markets, so that in either instance forward market cover is not available. In such cases, the state accepts responsibility for the exchange risk, thus ensuring that the project is undertaken. In essence, the government enables the project's sponsors and investors to concentrate on the non-exchange risks.

Such guarantees might be provided as a concession or a fee might be charged. In any event, the project's organisers know in advance their costs in terms of local currency. The guaranteeing organisation might be the state itself, a state-owned but self-financing body (for example, the Export Credit Guarantee Department in the UK guarantees long-term credits), or a private organisation. If it is the last named, it must have a good enough reputation – and sound enough finances – to be trusted as a guarantor. Note that the guaranteeing of exchange risk might be part of a wider package of export support guarantee: for example, against the blocking of payment by the importer's government (this is usually referred to as 'country risk'); it may, on the other hand, be only the exchange rate risk that is insured. These guarantees are of most use for covering transaction exposure.

Mention of risk guarantees should remind you of material you studied in Unit 5, Section 5.4.

Technique 5 Long-term borrowing in foreign currencies

This method – mainly used for reducing economic exposure – is simple yet effective. While in the past it was mainly open only to large well-known borrowers – IBM, ICI, Shell, and so on – competition in modern banking has ensured the development of techniques that enable almost any organisation to arrange loans in foreign currency, subject, of course, to any legal restrictions.

If a UK company has a Canadian factory, it can minimise CND economic exposure on its fixed assets by financing them with CND liabilities – a loan. Assuming the Canadian factory is mainly supplying its own domestic market, this method also helps to reduce the transaction exposure, at least from the subsidiary's viewpoint. Note, however, that it is usually difficult for a subsidiary to borrow 100% against its assets – lenders like to see some equity capital, even in 100%-owned subsidiaries of major foreign parents. If very high levels of gearing are seen in such subsidiaries it is quite common for the parent to have to stand as specific guarantor for the loans, rather than just offer its implicit support.

Exercise 7.2

In this case, how does a Canadian dollar loan taken out to provide a balance sheet hedge also aid in reducing transaction exposure?

Rearranging the group's loan portfolio can often be one of the most effective methods of reducing exposure. However, if it involves increasing the proportion of total borrowing that is in high-interest-rate currencies, the management must once again balance the costs and benefits. Also, a significant restructuring, should it be required, would probably require a board-level policy decision. You need also to bear in mind that such operations can, while reducing real exposure, actually create some apparent translation risk, depending on the particular accounting framework which applies. You saw an example of this type of situation in the reading about BBA plc in Section 2.3.

Incidentally, the increasing use of derivatives can add to this potential increase in apparent translation exposure; this is because many swaps are, at present, 'off-balance sheet', so the loan in a 'funny' currency appears on the balance sheet, but not the swap which 'converts' it into a currency actually usable by the borrower.

Swaps were covered in Unit 7, Section 8.

It is also now possible, using single-currency and/or cross-currency swaps, to separate the source of financing from the basis on which the organisation pays interest. If a UK organisation has a French subsidiary which generates EUR revenues, it may be possible to take out a GBP fixed-rate loan, and then swap the interest payments for this loan into EUR floating-rate interest payments. Thus the EUR interest payments can be matched against the EUR revenues.

Technique 6   Financial instruments

Once all other exposure reduction methods have been used (as much as is consistent with the organisation's hedging policy), the balance – which may be substantial – may require trading with the main forex products: spot and forward exchange transactions, or futures and options.

The latter – futures and options – are dealt with in the next unit; in fact you have read about interest rate futures in Unit 7, and the equivalents for foreign exchange are very close analogues. Here we look more closely at forward contracts. In Section 3 we covered how to calculate spot rates, cross rates and forward margins.

The simple forward contract is very easy to obtain in most major currencies and has the merit of being simple as a means of hedging currency exposure. However, there are many variations on the traditional forward contract which are on offer by banks; for example, an optional date forward contract, where the precise maturity date is left open. Forward contracts are one of the main external means of hedging foreign exchange exposure; it is therefore worth considering the advantages and disadvantages of using forward currency contracts to hedge exposure v. spot v. borrowing/deposit in the two currencies.

Sometimes there is not a readily available forward market, and it can be necessary to create a **synthetic forward**. This is no more than actually undertaking the transactions implied by the 'round the rectangle' idea. Remembering the equivalence, described in Section 4, between borrowing, lending and outright forward exchange rates, it is possible to replicate the effect of a forward purchase or sale by borrowing, lending and trading spot. It should be stressed that synthetic forwards are most common in cases where a minor currency – an exotic – is involved that does not support a 'deep' forward market, e.g. the Czech koruna. When using major currencies, it is almost always cheaper for non-financial organisations to book forward contracts directly. However, with the growth of investment in emerging markets there is now a greater demand for exotic currencies; in most such cases the bank will still be willing to quote a forward rate even when there is no external forward market. In fact it is undertaking to do the spot/borrow/lend set of transactions, and it is probably able to do so more cheaply than the customer – but it is often sensible to check whether the latter should actually do so itself.

The interest rate equivalent of a forward contract is a Forward Rate Agreement (FRA). This was discussed in Unit 7.

SUMMARY

Having identified and quantified exchange exposure in Section 2, in this part of the unit we have been concerned with ways of managing the risk caused by such exposure.

The techniques range from ones that involve just the managing organisation (internal methods) to those that are direct contracts with outside parties entered into solely for foreign exchange reasons (external methods). Exposure netting is an example of the former and a forward outright purchase contract an example of the latter. Between the two extremes are techniques that involve outside parties but are modifications to activities that would be conducted anyway; changing the currency of sales invoicing would be an example.

Some of the methods discussed provide a long-term elimination of exposure, for example matching foreign fixed assets with foreign loan liabilities. Such systems are particularly appropriate to control economic and translation exposure. On the other hand, they are less useful when dealing with the (typically) shorter-term and more variable elements of transaction exposure. As organisations go about their normal activities the levels of transaction exposure will continually change; it consequently needs to be managed in a more active way. For example, a UK company could have potential large exposure linked to a EUR sales contract; the exposure could initially be reduced by also sourcing as much as possible in EUR, and the exchange rate could be fixed on the balance sheet by selling EUR forward.

8 CREDIT RISK AND SETTLEMENT RISK

This section contains the discussion of settlement risk and credit risk, which are typically lumped together in this context under the heading '**trade risk**'. The two are combined in one section because they arise from the same root; indeed, settlement risk can sometimes be treated as (very) short-term credit risk. Also the risk profile is similar: low probability but danger of total loss.

When we look at credit risk, the intent is not to turn all B821 graduates into hardened credit analysts but to provide an introduction to the aspects of the subject with which all managers ought to be reasonably cognisant. As has been shown earlier, all organisations involved in business deals become trade credit bankers to their customers; to ignore this unpalatable fact is not managerially prudent. So, we will consider what signals you can look for to help decide whether a counterparty is a safe bet for the length of your normal trade terms.

Finally for this unit, we will look briefly at a range of products designed to help with the credit risk element of trade with distant parties: letters of credit (LCs) and letters of guarantee (LGs).

8.1 FUNDS TRANSFER AND SETTLEMENT RISK

An unexciting but important aspect of financial risk control which is relevant for almost any manager is the area of cash settlement. While the likelihood of funds going astray is usually small, the result of a mishap can be very serious. Financial institutions have taken 'settlement risk' seriously since the early 1970s (Box 8.1 explains why) and so should anyone responsible for transferring large amounts of money.

In general, the managerial responsibility is to devise and monitor a cash management system which does not constrain the organisation's activities while satisfying two key criteria:

(i) security of cash balances is protected

(ii) money is not left lying idle more than is absolutely necessary.

Large organisations will probably have a corporate treasury which acts as a payment service for the operating units, or at least has designed the cash system used. Unfortunately most businesses are not large enough to warrant such a specialist function, and so some knowledge of the standard rules for safe and efficient funds management is useful for any generalist manager.

BOX 8.1 HORRIBLE HERSTATT

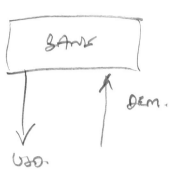

Banks have always had what they call 'settlement limits' for customers and other banks. This is supposed to put a ceiling on how much they will pay across to a counterparty on any particular day. However, until the 1970s such limits were often treated with scant respect, especially for foreign exchange trading. After all, by definition an exchange involves handing over and receiving equal value in two currencies, so where could there be a risk?

The Herstatt collapse showed rather graphically where the risk came from. Herstatt was a German bank which ran into trouble, and eventually collapsed. Up to the day of disaster, its foreign exchange dealers had bought large quantities of Deutschmarks for dollars, and on the final day the counterparties happily paid over their DEM – but the bank closed in the afternoon, which, given the time differential between Frankfurt and New York, was after the bank had received the DEM but before it had instructed its New York agent to pay the equivalent USD.

Oh, how they howled! The counterparty banks tried to claim that the DEM payments were inextricably linked to the USD receipts, and so they should be repaid. 'Not so' said the courts, and the banks were regarded the same as all other unsecured creditors. They eventually received a few cents on the dollar.

Since then, settlement risk has been taken seriously.

Clearly, managing cash and cash balances has an interest cost implication, as we discussed in the interest rate risk part of Unit 7. Here we are concerned with systems designed to ensure security is maintained over the money itself.

The basic rules, described in Box 8.2, are straightforward and should be common sense to any business person, but that does not mean they are always followed. If Barings Bank's senior management had applied them properly, a Singapore-based employee – one Mr Leeson – would not have been able in 1995 to lose £700 million of the shareholders' investment through futures and options trading.

It is important to realise that these ideas concerning cash security are not just of interest to banks or financial institutions but should be put into practice by any organisation that has to transfer funds in and out of its accounts. The bigger the company the larger and more diverse are likely to be the payments and receipts made, but such transfers, and their control, are important to companies of any size. If the rules required technical resources or expertise then it would be reasonable to ask for their use only in bigger businesses, but as they are really just codifying commonsense precautions it is fair to apply them to all organisations.

It is important to remember that most of the time the rules will be protecting you from losses caused by inadvertent mistakes rather than by deliberate fraud. Having a secure system that keeps a continuous check on the personnel involved is not a signal that you mistrust your people. It is the financial equivalent of a guard-rail at the cliff's edge.

An example of this is the modern practice for banks to record all phone calls made from the dealing room; any disagreement over a deal can quickly be traced, and usually that sorts the problem out immediately. It was succinctly put in a novel by Larry Niven: 'A verbal contract is as legally binding as the tape it's recorded on.'

BOX 8.2   BASIC RULES FOR CASH SETTLEMENT

(i)   The persons responsible for promulgating a contract and settling/accounting for it must be different. (This was the key Barings failing – Leeson controlled the trading *and* the 'back office'.)

The 'back office' is more properly called the Settlements Department; in practice it includes whoever is responsible for administering transactions after the dealers have had their wicked way ...

(ii)   For phone transactions, a different member of staff from the transactor should re-confirm the details as soon as possible, ensuring that both parties agree about what has been contracted. The different voice is important to avoid any repetition of an error caused, for example, by misinterpreting an accent – same person, same error possibly.

(iii)   Payments of significant amounts should require two signatures, preferably of senior personnel.

(iv)   Strict limits must be set in advance for the maximum amount that can be transferred to any one counterparty on any one day.

(v)   Where possible, legal title to goods or money should be retained until confirmed receipt of payment. So cleared funds in your account, not just a pretty cheque!

(vi)   Reconcile bank accounts as soon as and as frequently as possible.

(vii)   Protect carefully security codes and/or cash transfer stationery. Use numbered forms, and keep a check that none go missing – including 'mistakes'.

(viii)   Investigate discrepancies as a matter of urgency. Even where they are genuine errors (which is most of the time), the quicker they are corrected the lower will be the cost of so doing.

8.2   CREDIT ANALYSIS

This section draws and expands on the credit analysis section in Unit 3.

While not specialist loan assessors, most managers do need at times to be able to make sensible judgements about the granting of trade credit to customers.

Since we are talking about trade credit, it is reasonable to assume that we are concerned with short-term exposures, probably of the order of 30–60 days. This is based on 'normal trade terms' of 30 days, plus a little bit for the typical short delay often experienced.

Of course this time span only refers to a single invoiced amount. If you are a regular supplier it is possible, indeed probable, that your total exposure to a particular client is many times the average amount of a single debt. What is important is how much money is at risk for how long, should circumstances require you to withdraw further credit facilities.

If the accounts are computerised, and keep track of payment dates, why not program the machine to print, on request, a 'customer gap chart' (as in Unit 7) showing immediately the exposure situation?

How should you judge credit-worthiness? The techniques for accounts analysis dealt with in Units 2 and 3, and in your preceding studies, are just as valid here as when considering an equity or long-term debt investment. Indeed, the situation here is usually somewhat easier as you are only exposed for short periods at a time.

If we look at the simplistic but useful block diagram of the balance sheet (Figure 8.1), it reminds us of where we stand as creditors – the higher up in the 'liability' column the better. It is drawn up in order of payment in the case of liquidation, which is rather different from the usual balance sheet ordering.

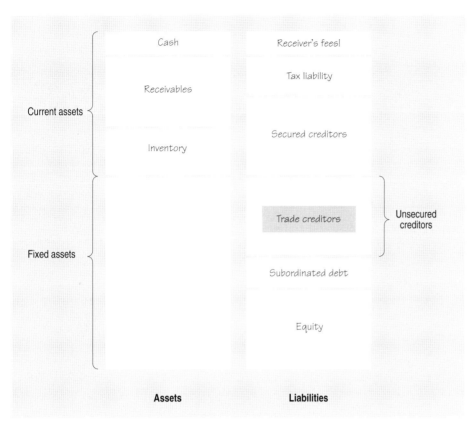

Figure 8.1   Diagrammatic representation of the balance sheet in the context of a liquidation

As can be seen, although in a going concern trade creditors tend to get paid as a matter of relative urgency (to avoid loss of credit privileges), this is no longer the case if the customer becomes bankrupt. We are then ranked along with all the other unsecured creditors; this can be quite well down the 'pecking order', especially if many of the fixed assets are pledged as security, for example a mortgage on the land and buildings. Thus it is necessary to consider to some extent the value of the whole business, using the analysis techniques from earlier in the course, and not just assume payment out of current cash flows.

However, this is looking at things in a 'worst case scenario' way. In practice most of the time we can expect to be paid in the normal course of trade, i.e. out of revenues derived by the customer from the sale of its goods and/or services. In other words, as current liability creditors we should be looking to the quality of the customer's current assets as our main surety of payment. All the usual points apply, for example:

- Is the company turning over satisfactorily?
- Is the inventory current and moving?
- What is the length of the operating cycle?
- Does the company strip out bad debts from its receivables conscientiously?
- Does the business have sufficient lines of short-term credit – other than us, the trade creditors?

- What is the customer's payment record with us and/or its reputation in the industry?

Where can you get answers to these and the other questions you should be asking? It is possible – indeed probably prudent – to request a credit report from the client's bank (with permission) or from an agency such as Dun and Bradstreet, but do not rely too much on the results you receive. It is important to remember that the bank has a duty of care to its customer, though it must not tell fibs to you, and therefore is likely to give so anodyne an answer as to be practically useless. Banks actually teach (to be precise, they used to – and I suspect they do so still) their staff how to word a true but unrevealing credit report so that neither the inquirer nor their customer could call them to account! For similar fears of litigation, credit agencies' reports are not much more illuminating, though they will certainly warn you of any court proceedings lodged against the prospective customer.

For example, Experian, as mentioned in Block 2.

Thus you should obtain reports from banks or agencies, but these should not be regarded as a substitute for your own analysis of the customer's balance sheet and income statement. No client who is serious about maintaining a continuing supplier/customer relationship with you will object to a request for the published accounts; indeed, many companies see such requests as contributory evidence that the supplier is professional and safe to rely on for ongoing supply of materials. Clearly, this is not sensible effort for a one-off minor order, and usually such transactions are done with the corporate fingers crossed, or on a cash payment basis.

An important source of information that is often overlooked by accounts departments – who are seldom as in touch with the market as are the operating units – is the industry 'grapevine' or the local Chamber of Commerce. If a business is having trouble, its peers are usually the first to find out, excepting perhaps the unfortunate firm's bank. Of course, such data is hearsay, perhaps even merely gossip, but it is unwise to ignore such rumours without at least trying to substantiate them.

Finally, institutions such as the CIFC (Company for Inter-Firm Comparisons) can be helpful. They give access to members to look at other members' accounting information, and to compare it within the peer group. To join you must lodge your own financial data – it is a quid pro quo system – but it is often a quicker way of getting accounts data than asking for annual reports, and is in a partially pre-digested form.

Exercise 8.1

Is the aim of trade credit analysis to reduce bad debts to zero?

Before we leave the subject of credit analysis, here is a cautionary tale to show that you need to think through the implications of your methods, and especially when introducing new techniques. The story in Box 8.3 is not strictly a trade credit example, but it is certainly relevant to business debt in a wider sense.

BOX 8.3   NEURAL NETWORKS AND CREDIT ANALYSIS

In the last few years work on 'artificial intelligence' in general, and 'neural networks' in particular, has developed the breed very considerably.

What is a neural network? Briefly (and superficially!) it is a type of computer designed to mimic the workings of a brain. What you do is feed in a large amount of data together with the results associated with that data, and over time the machine programs its own internal 'pathways' so that input corresponds with appropriate output, in a similar way to how neurones in the brain develop connections and pathways as we learn.

When the output from test data reliably matches the expected result, the machine is ready. You then feed it new data to get real results that were not pre-calculated. Astonishingly (at least to us lay people) the outputs of such machines tend to be faster and more accurate than from 'normal' computers.

What does this have to do with credit analysis? Some financial institutions in the USA realised that the type of analysis being done to decide on credit ratings was very amenable to neural network-type programming. Accordingly, they 'trained' neural computers with large amounts of data about past credit decisions and the eventual repayment outcomes. When the reliability of the results from the network exceeded the previous scoring methods in predicting whether a particular application should be accepted or rejected, they started to use it 'for real'.

Unfortunately, after a while the banks found themselves subject to a number of lawsuits. US law requires banks to give fair and careful consideration to any and all loan proposals. Bear in mind that in the USA being turned down for credit by one institution can have a very damaging 'knock-on' effect – embarrassing as an individual, potentially very serious as a small business.

The crux of the matter was that, while no one (well, not many people) doubted the neural networks were on average more accurate, it was impossible to prove that in any particular case 'due consideration' had been given. With a neural network you just feed in data at the front, say the magic word, and use the output from the back; it is the ultimate statistical 'black box'.

Since the banks could not show in a deterministic way why they had turned down the loans, they lost the cases. So now they have gone back to their previous assessment methods; they may be less accurate, but at least the banks can show that A, B and C were done and the answer was F – for 'Fail'.

8.3   CREDIT RISK TOOLS FOR INTERNATIONAL TRADE

A very important set of tools for reducing the credit uncertainties inherent in international trade is the various forms of letters of credit (LC). It is helpful for any manager who may become involved with importing or exporting to have some generalist understanding of the main types and their various advantages and disadvantages. Given the continuing internationalisation of business, it is likely that most B821 students will from time to time have to deal with some form of cross-border order. An overview knowledge of LCs should help to optimise the transaction formalities, to the benefit of both customer and supplier.

An example of a typical letter of credit is shown in Figure 8.2 opposite.

Irrevocable Documentary Credit Application

Applicant:	Issuing Bank:

Date of Application:

☐ Issue by (air) mail   ☐ with brief advice by teletransmission (see UCP 500 Article 11)

☐ Issue by teletransmission (see UCP 500 Article 11)

☐ Transferable Credit-as per UCP 500 Article 48

Expiry Date and Place for Presentation of Documents
Expiry Date:
Place for Presentation:

Beneficiary:

Confirmation of the Credit:

☐ not requested   ☐ requested   ☐ authorised if requested by Beneficiary

Partial shipments ☐ allowed   ☐ not allowed

Transhipments ☐ allowed   ☐ not allowed

Please refer to UCP 500 transport Articles for exceptions to this condition

☐ Insurance will be covered by us

Amount in figures and words (Please use ISO Currency codes)

Credit available with Nominated Bank:

☐ by payment at sight
☐ by deferred payment at:
☐ by acceptance of drafts at:
☐ by negotiation

Shipment as defined in UCP 500 Article 46
From:
For transportation to:
Not later than:

Against the documents detailed herein:
☐ and Beneficiary's draft(s) drawn on:

Goods (Brief description without excessive details - see UCP 500 Article 5):

Terms:
☐ FAS   ☐ CIF
☐ FOB   ☐ Other terms:
☐ CFR   ☐ as per INCOTERMS

Commercial invoice ☐ signed, original and ☐ copies

Transport Document:
☐ Multimodal Transport Document, covering at least two different modes of transport
☐ Marine/Ocean Bill of Lading covering a port-to-port shipment
☐ Non-Negotiable Sea Waybill covering a port-to-port shipment
☐ Air Waybill, original for the consignor
☐ Other transport document:
☐ to the order of
☐ endorsed in blank
☐ marked freight ☐ prepaid ☐ payable at destination
☐ notify:

Insurance Document:
☐ policy ☐ Certificate ☐ Declaration under an open cover. Covering the following risks:

Certificates:
☐ Origin
☐ Analysis
☐ Health
☐ Other

Other Documents:
☐ Packing List
☐ Weight List

Documents to be presented within ☐ days after the date of shipment but within the validity of the Credit.

Additional Instructions:

We request you to issue on our behalf and for our account your irrevocable Credit in accordance with the above instructions (marked (x) where appropriate).

This Credit will be subject to the Uniform Customs and Practice for Documentary Credits (1993 Revision, Publication No. 500 of the International Chamber of Commerce, Paris, France), insofar as they are applicable.

_____
Name and signature of the Applicant

Consult the Issuing Bank for guidance if the completion of this form should raise any question

Figure 8.2   A letter of credit

Letters of credit

What is a **letter of credit**? In essence it is a way of reducing uncertainty about payment from trade transactions by interposing one or more banks between the transacting parties, as shown in Box 8.4. Incidentally, LCs are sometimes called **documentary credits**, because they are concerned with the documents – such as invoice, bill of exchange, bill of lading, certificate of origin – involved with a trade deal rather than the goods themselves. Banks like processing paper, not products!

The choices available under the documentary credits system are extensive – there are over 140 main variants – and are defined by the rules laid out in ICC500 by the International Chambers of Commerce. We will not, I am sure you will be glad to read, go into detail about each of them, but it is worth looking at the basic options dependent on three factors:

- who is 'on risk'
- when will the supplier receive funds
- when will the customer pay.

The first choice that must be made is whether the LC will be 'revocable' or 'irrevocable'. This means whether or not the customer can, with due notice, cancel the LC before the goods are shipped – strictly, before the documents are received by the advising bank. This does not give much assurance to the 'beneficiary' (S), especially if the goods are customised to fit the order, so 'irrevocable' LCs are much the more common. With such a beast, provided the terms and conditions are met – which usually includes a last date, for the protection of the buyer – the supplier can be reassured about receiving payment. If you are ever the beneficiary of an LC, make sure that it has the word 'irrevocable' on it before you accept it!

Once a letter of credit has been set up, S – the 'beneficiary' – has transferred its credit risk from exposure to the 'customer' (C) to that of the 'opening' or 'issuing' bank. In general this is a substantial improvement, since banks are normally regulated so as to ensure their financial stability. Mind you, BCCI's main business was trade finance and documentary credits – but it is fair to say that the fall from grace of that institution was the exception rather than the rule. However, it is worth pointing out that the right to payment under the LC does not remove S's rights to claim directly from C; this may be important if C is, say, a very good risk (e.g. a state institution or Ford or IBM) which may be better than the local bank issuing the LC. Thus a documentary credit is always an enhancement of credit quality, though this may not necessarily be the main impetus for its creation.

BCCI was an international bank which accepted deposits in the UK and Pakistan but went bankrupt in 1991.

There is nothing particular about Russia, it just happens to be a pertinent example at the time of writing. At other times, other choices could have been made (such as the Philippines in 1983 or Ecuador in 1999).

BOX 8.4   WHY A LETTER OF CREDIT?

Let us suppose that a company, call it S for 'supplier', is negotiating a significant order with company C, for 'customer', but is concerned about granting credit terms as the two have not transacted before. Furthermore, C is based in, say, Russia, a country which has recently had well-publicised difficulties in terms of foreign currency availability.

S could remove its credit risk by demanding payment before shipment from C, but that might jeopardise the whole deal, C not being in a position to pay 'up front'. In any case, C has little knowledge about S's financial position, so would be reluctant to pay before receipt of goods.

How can this be resolved? By using the international system of letters of credit to set up an agreement for goods and funds flow that reassures both C and S. It allows each of them to deal with an entity known to them and (hopefully) one that is regarded as financially sound – usually their own banks.

Once C and S have agreed the trade terms of their contract, C requests its bank to open an LC in favour of S. This will state precisely what funds will be paid, and when, by the bank upon their receipt of a specified set of documents. S is thus taking the credit risk of the bank rather than of C, which is usually an improvement. Vice versa, C is assured that payment will not be made unless the proper paperwork (bills of lading showing that goods are actually shipped, certificates of quality that they meet the agreed specification, etc.) has been received by the bank. This is shown in Figure 8.3.

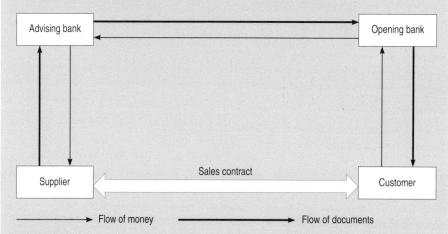

Figure 8.3

S can further improve the surety of its receipt of funds by asking for the 'advising' bank – often its own branch – to add its 'confirmation' to the LC. Provided S supplies the correct documents at the right time, the confirming bank in S's own country will guarantee to pay on the due date. Thus the bank has assumed any country risk of C's homeland preventing the bank in that country completing the transfer of funds, for example by imposing a foreign exchange freeze.

Clearly, C and S have to pay for the services and assurance they receive, but the reduction in uncertainty is usually perceived to be well worth the banks' fees.

But, as described in Box 8.4, sometimes S will want to bring the residual risk it is taking as close to home as possible. It can then request that the LC be 'confirmed' rather than just 'advised'. 'Confirmation' adds the guarantee of the bank in S's country (often its own bank) to that of the issuing bank in C's country. This may be requested for any or all of three reasons:

(i)   S may not know enough about the issuing bank to be happy to rely on its credit-worthiness

(ii) S may be concerned that country risk problems may prevent the issuing bank from paying, even if it tries to

(iii) S may wish to bring the contract within the jurisdiction of its own country's laws.

Usually the cost of adding its own bank's guarantee is borne by the beneficiary, so confirmation is by no means universal, particularly when the issuing bank is in a stable country. If the LC is 'advised' instead of 'confirmed', the bank in S's location acts only as a checking and posting facility. This is still useful as it gives the exporter evidence that it has delivered documents in accordance with the terms of the LC – 'proof of posting', in effect.

The transfer of goods from supplier to customer inevitably takes time, and if the distance travelled is long so too may be the interval between dispatch and receipt. Someone has to fund the time-lag, and the terms for so doing are often specified as part of the LC process. The funding requirement can be taken up by any of the four protagonists, or split among them.

Perhaps the most common split is for the supplier to fund the shipping period and then be paid, but there are situations where it is agreed that the buyer has as much as six months' credit. Since the final payment is assured by the LC bank(s), the supplier can make a decision about this based solely on its cost of funding the deal – the guarantee has removed any payment worries about granting extended credit. At the other extreme, in some cases the buyer even helps fund the supplier's production period; here the buyer is accepting increased risk between the time of sending money and the advising bank receiving the shipping documents. This is a fairly rare sort of deal these days, but may be used where there is a substantial difference between the cost of borrowing for the supplier and the buyer – a historical example is described in Box 8.5.

BOX 8.5   A RED-LETTER LC CAUSING A RED-LETTER DAY?

In the nineteenth and early twentieth centuries most of the wool grown on Australian sheep was spun and woven in English mills, a situation where large, credit-worthy companies were buying from numerous individual suppliers, and where the time between contract and delivery would typically be up to nine months.

It became traditional for the English buyer to open a red-letter LC in favour of its farming supplier whereby it paid for the wool up to six months before receiving the bales at its mill. Of course, the price paid was reduced to reflect the effective loan period, but this was a cheaper form of borrowing for most Australian farmers than their trying to raise the funds on their own credit-worthiness.

It is not recorded how the farmers greeted the news that the year's red-letter LC had been received from England, but it is possible to speculate!

To be precise, the official title of this type of LC was 'red clause', because the key clauses were written in red. However, since all the relevant words were in red the colloquial name was indeed 'red letter' – and 'red clause' spoils the story!

The example may seem to be a little old, but in fact similar arrangements are even now used in the international agriculture business, because it is still an industry where (relatively) small producers are regular suppliers to large purchasers. In many such cases the legal framework of documentary credits is used even for national trade, this being easier than designing a loan agreement from scratch.

The fundamental point is that it is always good business practice for the parties to a contract to arrange funding such that overall the least amount of interest has to be paid. The assurance of payment given by an LC allows this funding decision to be separated from the problem of granting credit. Incidentally, it is not automatically the larger party to the contract, or even the more financially sound, which can raise funds most cheaply. For example, there may be state-subsidised export financing available; very often discounting a bill of exchange drawn under an export LC is the most convenient way of accessing such a source (the LC system assures the state provider that the subsidy is only applied to exports).

Lastly, even if the beneficiary does not receive funding through the LC itself, the process usually provides it with a bill of exchange accepted by a bank for payment on the due date. This can be used to raise money as and when required, either by discounting the bill directly or by using it as collateral for a loan.

Letters of guarantee

A cousin of the LC is the LG – **letter of guarantee**. This allows for automatic payment if specific terms of a contract are not fulfilled, for example failing to supply or supplying goods that do not meet set quality criteria.

Just as a supplier is at risk of not receiving payment having fulfilled its side of a contract, so can the purchaser be risking substantial financial loss if the seller fails to supply to specification and on time. For a large project, even before a contract is granted, the client is justified in requesting surety that the bidders are serious and can undertake the work if selected.

In such cases the supplier will request its bank to open an LG in favour of the customer. This will state that if certain events occur – e.g. the project is completed late, the work fails a safety inspection – a pre-set amount will be paid by the bank to the aggrieved buyer. Thus the bank, not the customer, is taking the credit risk for reparation in the event of misadventure.

Particularly for large capital projects, an LG-type instrument provides the buyer with assurance of completion in a similar way to the LC assuring the supplier of payment. There are numerous names used for this type of document; for example, 'bid bond', 'performance bond', 'completion guarantee'. Legally, these instruments are developments of letters of guarantee, being more precise about the specific events which can trigger payment. Nevertheless, they are all products of a similar type dealing with similar needs – bid/performance/completion bonds can be regarded as specialist 'offspring' of the generalist LG.

A very important point concerning both letters of guarantee and letters of credit is that the banks are only concerned with documents, not reality. This may seem like ultimate pedantry, but it has caused grief to many managers over the years – a salutary example is described in Box 8.6. But the documentary credit process solves many more problems than it causes.

BOX 8.6   BRIDGE? WHAT BRIDGE?

This cautionary tale is sufficiently old (1970s vintage) that it is unlikely to cause offence to name the countries involved.

A British engineering firm won a major commission to build an important bridge in Libya. Both sides were happy about the price and terms of the contract, including LCs for stage payments for the British builder and LGs concerning timely completion to protect the Libyan customer. These were duly opened in favour of the appropriate beneficiaries.

To reduce the adverse impact on the country's balance of payments, the amount of imported materials was restricted. In particular, the large quantities of cement needed were to be purchased from a local state-owned Libyan cement factory.

Unfortunately the factory was unable to supply the proper material, either with regard to volume or quality. The British company requested that it be allowed to import the required cement so that it could build the bridge. This was refused by the relevant ministry.

Not having access to the necessary raw materials, the builder was unable to complete the contract on time. The customer presented documents certificating non-compliance to the LG bank, and was paid the forfeit amounts – debited, of course, from the British company's bank account.

Feeling somewhat hard done by, the builder sued the bank in the UK courts, claiming that the non-completion was not their fault and the bank should not have paid. The judgement went against the contractor, since the letter of guarantee made no mention of cement supply as a required pre-condition for claiming – even though the effective owner of the non-supplying cement factory was the same entity as the customer claiming under the guarantee.

SUMMARY

Notwithstanding the preceding example – which was a failure to draw up the right agreements rather than a flaw in the documentary credit system – the use of LCs and LGs have done a great deal in a practical way to encourage the expansion of international trade seen particularly since the Second World War. It is not necessary for each manager to be an expert on the peculiarities of the various forms of these products, but all should have a basic understanding of what they are for and how they are used. All banks that operate in the documentary credit field will have the expertise to help to construct an LC properly, but you cannot assume that such knowledge is available in every branch – it is often concentrated in the larger offices. This is even more true of letters of guarantee, which are less common and usually less 'standard' than a letter of credit. The foregoing warning notwithstanding, both types of instrument are designed to be straightforward and it is perfectly realistic for a business which opens or receives LCs reasonably regularly to build internal expertise to a level at least as good as that of a bank.

Before any readers claim that they have no use for such an international product, let them consider how they would deal with an opportunity to supply a large order on 180 days' credit to a new customer 300 miles away they knew not from Adam – or who was known, with negative feelings, by the accounts department. Or perhaps they wished to bid for a major contract, but had to provide a 'bid bond' along with the offer? A documentary credit can be helpful in any trade contract, national or international, and understanding what is available for which situations ought to be part of a modern manager's knowledge-base.

SUMMARY AND CONCLUSIONS

In this unit, we have attempted to introduce you to many aspects of foreign exchange and credit management. We first looked at how foreign exchange exposure can be defined, identified and measured. From that, you will now be aware that there are three types of foreign exchange exposure – transaction, translation and economic exposure. We then provided you with some simple approaches that can help you measure the degree of transaction exposure and, to some extent, economic exposure. We went on to look at the foreign exchange market in general and then at some of the basic terminology of foreign exchange so that you could gain some familiarity with such terms as premiums and discounts, spot, and forward contracts. You gained some familiarity with the foreign exchange information given in the *Financial Times*.

The following section then looked at some of the more theoretical and pragmatic approaches to forecasting future exchange rates. You learnt how important forecasting future exchange rates can be for decisions about how to deal with foreign exchange exposure, and the different approaches to forecasting foreign exchange rates – including the approach which takes an EMH view and says don't bother to forecast!

In the next section we reviewed some of the practical arguments for and against hedging foreign exchange exposure, and how exposure management might be organised.

In Section 7, we looked at six of the standard approaches to hedging foreign exchange exposure. You learnt that it is best, usually, to look at possible internal techniques of hedging (netting and matching being examples) before looking at external techniques (such as forward contracts).

The final section of the unit then turned to another aspect of financial risk, namely trade risk. Even though in total this is a very different topic from foreign exchange, we looked at two aspects which are quite closely involved with the world of forex. Settlement risk applies more broadly than just to foreign exchange deals, but they are certainly a pertinent source of potential problems. The other area considered was letters of credit and letters of guarantee – two products crucial to the business of international trade.

The third aspect considered was that of trade credit. All managers are, at times, bankers. As soon as you do anything other than demand cash payment for all goods or services provided, you are also providing a short-term loan facility; it is not expected that busy people will waste significant time as junior credit analysts, but a basic understanding of what to look for and where to look is a useful skill for a modern manager.

Objectives

At the end of this unit, you should now be able to:

- use a spot currency quotation for buying or selling currencies
- calculate a forward exchange rate
- describe the linkage between forward exchange rates and interest rates
- describe some of the determinants of exchange rate variability
- calculate net foreign exchange exposure
- explain the difference between transaction, translation and economic exposure
- design a hedging strategy to control foreign exchange risk
- know where to find and how to use information for making trade credit decisions
- implement the key rules for managing the security of cash balances and funds transfer
- understand the main types of and uses for documentary credits.

ANSWERS TO EXERCISES

Exercise 2.1

Issues such as price sensitivity and overall competition in the market will determine whether Apres GmbH can pass on such cost increases.

Exercise 3.1

It means that 83% of foreign exchange transactions are for financial reasons (e.g. taking a position on a currency) or speculation rather than to do directly with underlying trade activities. Note that this is not necessarily a bad thing as it ensures that there is a very liquid market to which 'trade transactors' have access whenever they need to complete a deal with their banks or other financial intermediaries.

Exercise 4.1

Follow the same procedure: 'buy' USD with GBP and then 'sell' USD for CHF. So 'buy' USD1.6324 with each GBP, and 'buy' CHF1.4915 with each USD, giving 1.6324 × 1.4915 = 2.4347 CHF for each GBP, i.e. CHF2.4347/ GBP1 is the calculated cross rate. If you compare this with the figure given in Table 4.1, it is the same, as you would expect.

Exercise 4.2

There is no difference at all. The two statements are equivalent.

Exercise 4.3

The answer is that, as the US interest rate is lower, you would expect the USD to appreciate against the GBP, and therefore the GBP would purchase fewer USD in a year.

Exercise 4.4

$$\text{Annual forward margin} = \frac{(\text{Spot} - \text{Forward}) \times 360 \times 100}{\text{Spot} \times n}$$

$$= \frac{(1.60 - 1.57) \times 360 \times 100}{1.60 \times 360}$$

$$= 1.875\%$$

Exercise 4.5

No. As long as the forward rates are in line with the interest rates, there should be no significant difference between the first two alternatives. So we can effectively ignore the spot + deposit/borrowing choice. The third option relies on using the spot rate in one month's time. This is fundamentally different from the other two options, as the cost of the third option is not known with certainty. The forward rate is the market's best estimate of what the future spot rate will be, but it is only an estimate. The third option could end up costing considerably more than the others.

Exercise 5.1

GBP100 in one year, at an annual interest rate of 13% = GBP113

USD150 in one year, at an annual interest rate of 10% = USD165

Therefore forward rate in one year = USD165/GBP113 = USD1.46 = GBP1.

Exercise 5.2

Although superficially the median predictions seem quite accurate, closer examination shows rather poorer results.

To start with, use of an averaged statistic (strictly the median – the middle forecast – is an average but not the one we typically regard as the average, i.e. the mean) will tend to flatter the forecasts. Oddly enough, this effect is stronger the more independent the different forecasts are; but the chartists are all supposed to be looking for the same things in the same data, so should come up with similar analyses. However, the article states that there were wide variations in the predictions, so the benefits of averaging become significant!

While the previous point is a rather esoteric (but valid) statistical factor that you are not expected to know, a quite clear effect can be seen just from looking at the graphs. The predicted rates lag the actual by about the forecast period – the chart forecasts do little more (on average) than say that the rates will not change much over a week or four weeks. That is on the whole about right – but we do not need an expensive chartist's prediction to use that as a forecast.

The graphs shown do not really offer much good evidence for or against the accuracy of the chartists' forecasts, and we also do not know how much of their individual analyses was influenced by fundamental as opposed to technical factors.

With regard to the efficient markets hypothesis, the article's evidence neither conflicts nor agrees with the hypothesis. As said in the preceding paragraph, the graphs do not show that the chartists' forecasts are any more accurate than a simple strategy of predicting that the near-future spot will be little different from today's rate. If there was clear evidence of accurate chartist predictions, then there would be an a priori conflict with EMH, since it holds that past price data (known to everybody) should not carry information about future price movements.

Even then, the conflict could be resolved by finding that the forecasters were in fact using significant amounts of economic fundamental analysis instead of relying solely on past chart data.

Finally, it is important always to remember that tests of EMH normally use closing or other periodic price records, and with this sort of data the evidence for the hypothesis is strong. For example, corporate treasurers, investment managers and civil servants all operate in the sort of time-frame in which EMH holds; market makers and currency speculators work on a minute-by-minute time horizon, and for those participants technical analysis may be valuable. As the article says, the majority of them take 'the charts' into account if for no other reason than they know that their competitors are doing so.

This difference in outlook is most clearly shown by the forecasting period chosen for the survey: one week and four weeks. To a treasurer, six months is quite soon – to a foreign exchange trader, four weeks is the very long-term.

Exercise 6.1

Because there is no expected gain or loss compared to leaving open the position, and since it reduces the currency risk to zero, it must be the optimum risk/return strategy.

Exercise 6.2

If you only invoice in your home currency, e.g. a French company invoicing into the UK always invoices in EUR, then you are passing on the currency risk to your customers. This might lead to the loss of competitive advantage with local currency suppliers.

Exercise 7.1

By buying and selling in GBP – its domestic currency. Of course, requiring that it be charged in GBP rather than USD might in itself be quite costly, since the non-UK supplier is likely now to set the price to include the exchange risk that is being taken on.

Exercise 7.2

If the factory is selling to the local market, its revenue will be mostly in CND; if the loan taken to finance the operations is also in CND, the interest and principal expenses will be in the same currency as the revenue, reducing the subsidiary's exposure.

Exercise 8.1

Not really. While you should strive in each case to be accurate in granting or withholding credit, on an overall basis it is important to accept that it is not a precise science. If you have no bad debts over a period of time, it is likely that you are applying too harsh a set of criteria – and are turning away a lot of good business to weed out the last few miscreants.

APPENDIX   PROOF OF FORWARD MARGIN FORMULA

Consider two currencies, F and L, that are connected by the spot rate, S, such that $S \times L = F$.

Let us assume that there is also a forward outright rate, that is the rate applicable for exchange deals delivering after a period of t days. It can be written as $S + FM$, where FM is the forward margin.

Lastly, assume that the interest rate for currency F for a period of t days is $i(F)$, and that for currency L is $i(L)$. Both currencies are Eurocurrencies where interest is calculated on the basis of the actual number of days divided by 360 (a financial market custom).

You have today an amount P of currency L that needs to be invested for t days.

What can you do? You have two choices.

(i) Invest the money for t days in L at the relevant interest rate, $i(L)$.

(ii) Sell currency L now and invest for t days in currency F at $i(F)$; at the same time book a forward outright purchase of currency L for an amount matching the proceeds of the currency F investment.

If one route were more profitable than the other, an arbitrage opportunity would exist (either you could borrow F and invest L by selling/buying F, or vice versa – whichever was profitable) and trading would take place until the discrepancy was eliminated. So method (i) must equal method (ii), that is:

$$P \times (1 + (i(L) \times t)/360) = P \times (S/\text{Forward rate})$$
$$\times (1 + (i(F) \times t)/360)$$

The Ps cancel out; multiplying both sides by the Forward rate and remembering that Forward rate $= S + FM$ we get:

$$(S + FM) \times (1 + (i(L) \times t)/360) = S \times (1 + (i(F) \times t)/360)$$

Multiplying through by 360, subtracting S from both sides, and collecting all the remaining S terms on the right-hand side:

$$FM \times (360 + (i(L) \times t) = S \times ((i(F) \times t) - (i(L) \times t))$$
$$= S \times t \times (i(F) - i(L))$$

Dividing through by the left-hand side factor, we have the result required:

$$FM = (S \times t \times (i(F) - i(L))/(360 + (i(L) \times t))$$

REFERENCES AND FURTHER READING

Buckley, A. (1996) *Multinational Finance*, Prentice Hall.

Douch, W. (1988) *The Economics of Foreign Exchange: a practical market approach*, Woodhead-Faulkner.

Eiteman, D.K., Stonehill, A.I. and Moffett, M.H. (1995) *Multinational Business Finance*, Addison Wesley.

Kern, D. (1996) 'Tremors that spoil the distant view', *Corporate Finance*, September.

Shapiro, A. (1992) *Multinational Financial Management*, Allyn and Bacon.

Tygier, C. (1988) *Basic Handbook of Foreign Exchange: a guide to foreign exchange dealing*, second edition, Euromoney Publications.

Wood, D. and Bátiz-Lazo, Bernardo (1995) *Introduction to International Banking (Part I: Basic Concepts and Operations)*, Manchester Business School, mimeo.

ACKNOWLEDGEMENTS

Grateful acknowledgement is made to the following sources for permission to reproduce material in this unit:

Text

Box 2.2: 'Chemical reactions', *Financial Times*, 10 March 1993; *Box 2.3:* Courtesy of Allied Domecq PLC and EMI Group PLC; *Box 4.2:* 'Observer: Spot the ball', *Financial Times*, 22 January 1997; *Box 5.3:* 'Big MacCurrencies', *The Economist*, 11 April 1998, © The Economist, London 1998.

Figures

Figure 3.1: Courtesy of Standard Chartered PLC; *Figure 5.1:* Demirag, I. and Goddard, S. (1994) *Financial Management for International Business*, McGraw-Hill Publishing Company; *Figure 8.2: ICC Guide to Documentary Credit Operations for the UCP 500*, ICC Publication No. 515 – ISBN 92 842 1159 X Published in its official English version by the International Chamber of Commerce. Copyright © 1994 – International Chamber of Commerce (ICC), Paris. Available from: *ICC Publishing S.A.*, 38 Cours Albert 1er, 75008 Paris, France or from *ICC United Kingdom*, 14/15 Belgrave Square, London SW1X 8PS, United Kingdom.

Tables

Table 2.2: Buckley, A. 1996, *Multinational Finance*, Prentice Hall Europe; *Table 4.1:* 'Spot, forward against the pound', *Financial Times*, 7 August 1998.

Cartoons/Photographs

P. 6: © Evening Standard Company Ltd. Reproduction by permission; p. 10: © Tony Souter, The Hutchison Library; p. 16: Reprinted with permission from the creators from *Stockworth: An American CEO*, 1998; p. 20: © The Skyscan Photo Library; p. 36: © PowerStock/Zefa; p. 48: Kevin KAL Kallaugher, *The Baltimore Sun* 1989, *The Economist* 1997; p. 60: © Barry Smith.

B821 FINANCIAL STRATEGY

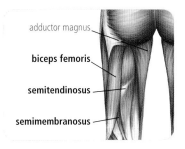

adductor magnus

biceps femoris

semitendinosus

semimembranosus

BEST FOR

- **semitendinosus**
- **semimembranosus**
- **biceps femoris**
- **vastus medialis**
- **vastus lateralis**
- **rectus femoris**

- **gluteus maximus**
- **gluteus medius**
- **piriformis**
- **erector spinae**
- **tibialis anterior**
- **tibialis posterior**

- **soleus**
- **gastrocnemius**
- **deltoideus medialis**
- **infraspinatus**
- **supraspinatus**
- **teres minor**

latissimus dorsi

obliquus externus

rectus abdominis

gluteus maximus

piriformis

obliquus internus*

gluteus medius*

tensor fasciae latae

vastus intermedius*

vastus lateralis

transversus abdominis*

adductor longus

tibialis posterior

rectus femoris

gracilis*

flexor hallucis*

erector spinae*

supraspinatus*

infraspinatus*

teres minor

deltoideus medialis

biceps brachii

triceps brachii

brachioradialis

sartorius

gastrocnemius

vastus medialis

soleus

tibialis anterior

peroneus

extensor hallucis*

ANNOTATION KEY

**Black text indicates
target muscles**

Grey text indicates other
working muscles

* indicates deep muscles

III

SWISS BALL REVERSE BRIDGE ROTATION

① Lie with your shoulders and lower back on a Swiss ball and your feet hip-width apart. Your knees should be bent at 90 degrees.

② Grasp a medicine ball with both hands, and position your arms straight up.

③ Rotate your upper body to the left, rolling onto your left shoulder on top of the Swiss ball.

④ Hold for 5 seconds, and then slowly roll back to the starting position with the Swiss ball in the centre of your shoulders.

TARGETS
• Obliques
• Abdominals

LEVEL
• Intermediate

BENEFITS
• Stabilises core
• Strengthens obliques and abdominals

NOT ADVISABLE IF YOU HAVE . . .
• Neck issues
• Lower-back pain

⑤ Repeat the exercise, rotating your torso and rolling your shoulders to the right.

AVOID
• Bending your arms.
• Continuing to rotate the Swiss ball when it is lying directly under one shoulder and both shoulders are vertical.

DO IT RIGHT
- Position the Swiss ball directly between your shoulder blades to start the exercise.
- Activate your abdominals so that you maintain neutral alignment.
- Keep your hips in line with your knees as you rotate your upper body, to work your spinal rotators.

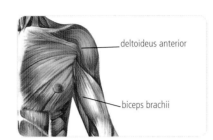

deltoideus anterior

biceps brachii

BEST FOR
- obliquus externus
- obliquus internus

ANNOTATION KEY
Black text indicates target muscles
Grey text indicates other working muscles
* indicates deep muscles

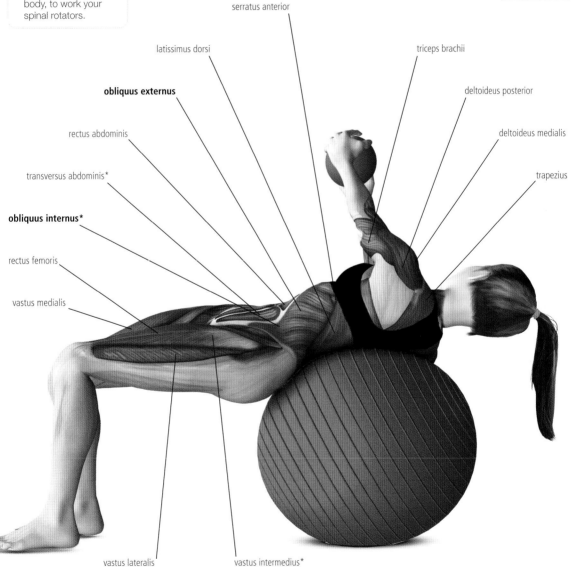

serratus anterior

latissimus dorsi

triceps brachii

obliquus externus

deltoideus posterior

rectus abdominis

deltoideus medialis

transversus abdominis*

trapezius

obliquus internus*

rectus femoris

vastus medialis

vastus lateralis

vastus intermedius*

SWISS BALL SITTING BALANCE

1 Sit on a Swiss ball with your feet together and your hands resting on the ball at your sides.

2 Lift one foot off the floor, and hold for 5 seconds.

3 Put your foot down, and then lift your other foot.

4 Repeat five times on each leg.

TARGETS
- Abdominals
- Quadriceps

LEVEL
- Beginner

BENEFITS
- Stabilises core
- Strengthens abdominals

NOT ADVISABLE IF YOU HAVE . . .
- Neck issues
- Lower-back pain

DO IT RIGHT
- Sit up straight, and keep your abdominals activated.

ANNOTATION KEY

Black text indicates target muscles

Grey text indicates other working muscles

* indicates deep muscles

iliopsoas*

pectineus*

- rectus abdominis
- transversus abdominis
- rectus femoris
- vastus lateralis
- vastus intermedius
- vastus medialis

rectus abdominis

tensor fasciae latae

transversus abdominis*

sartorius

vastus intermedius*

rectus femoris

vastus medialis*

vastus lateralis

AVOID
- Leaning forwards as you lift your leg.

SWISS BALL HIP CIRCLES

❶ Sit on a Swiss ball with your feet together and your hands on your hips.

DO IT RIGHT
• Keep your circles small—if you feel a crunching in your neck, you are moving too widely.

AVOID
• Using your legs to initiate the movement.

❷ Tighten your abdominal muscles, and use your pelvis to rotate the ball slowly to the right in small circles.

TARGETS
• Lower back
• Hips

LEVEL
• Beginner

BENEFITS
• Stabilises core
• Stretches lower back

NOT ADVISABLE IF YOU HAVE . . .
• Lower-back pain

❸ Return to the starting position, and repeat on the other side.

SWISS BALL HIP CIRCLES • CORE-TRAINING EXERCISES

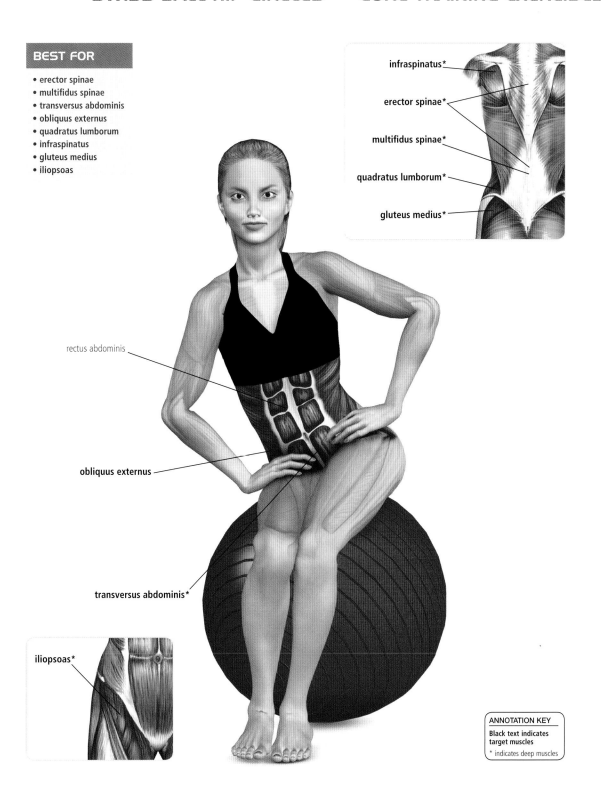

BEST FOR

- erector spinae
- multifidus spinae
- transversus abdominis
- obliquus externus
- quadratus lumborum
- infraspinatus
- gluteus medius
- iliopsoas

infraspinatus*

erector spinae*

multifidus spinae*

quadratus lumborum*

gluteus medius*

rectus abdominis

obliquus externus

transversus abdominis*

iliopsoas*

ANNOTATION KEY
Black text indicates target muscles
* indicates deep muscles

117

SWISS BALL REVERSE BRIDGE ROLL

❶ Lie with your lower back on a Swiss ball and your feet together. Your knees should be bent at 90 degrees. Position your arms out to the sides.

DO IT RIGHT
- Exhale as you roll on the ball, and inhale as you return to the starting position.
- Hold your body stable as you roll across the ball, working against the ball's natural rotation.
- Increase the space between your feet if necessary to maintain your balance.

TARGETS
- Obliques
- Abdominals

LEVEL
- Intermediate

BENEFITS
- Stabilises core
- Strengthens obliques and abdominals

NOT ADVISABLE IF YOU HAVE . . .
- Neck pain
- Lower-back pain

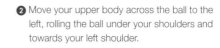

❷ Move your upper body across the ball to the left, rolling the ball under your shoulders and towards your left shoulder.

❸ Hold for 5 seconds, and then slowly roll the ball back to the centre of your shoulders.

❹ Return to the starting position, and then roll to the right. Repeat five times on each side.

AVOID
- Allowing your pelvis to drop out of alignment—your body should form a straight line from your shoulders to your knees.
- Continuing to rotate the ball when it is lying directly under one shoulder and both shoulders are vertical.

MODIFICATION

Easier: Rather than keeping your feet together, position them about shoulder-width apart. Then follow steps 2 through 4.

ANNOTATION KEY

Black text indicates target muscles

Grey text indicates other working muscles

* indicates deep muscles

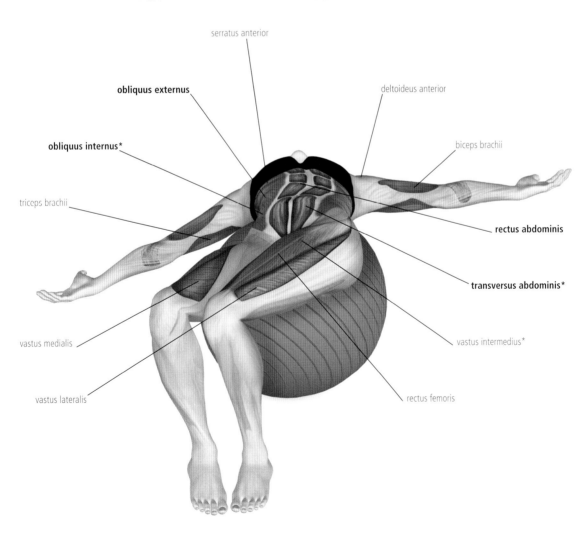

serratus anterior

obliquus externus

deltoideus anterior

obliquus internus*

biceps brachii

triceps brachii

rectus abdominis

transversus abdominis*

vastus medialis

vastus intermedius*

vastus lateralis

rectus femoris

ABDOMINAL HIP LIFT

1 Lie down with your legs in the air and crossed at the ankles, knees straight. Place your arms on the floor, straight by your sides.

DO IT RIGHT
- Keep your legs straight and firm throughout the exercise.
- Relax your neck and shoulders as you lift the hips.

AVOID
- Jerking your movements or using momentum to lift your hips.

BEST FOR

- rectus abdominis
- transversus abdominis
- vastus intermedius
- tensor fasciae latae
- gluteus maximus
- gluteus medius
- triceps brachii
- rectus femoris
- iliopsoas

TARGETS
- Abdominals
- Upper arms

LEVEL
- Intermediate

BENEFITS
- Strengthens core and pelvic stabilisers
- Firms and tones lower abdominals

NOT ADVISABLE IF YOU HAVE . . .
- Back pain
- Neck pain
- Shoulder pain

2 Pinching your legs together and squeezing your buttocks, press into the back of your arms to lift your hips upwards.

3 Slowly return your hips to the floor. Repeat 10 times, then switch with the opposite leg crossed in the front.

quadratus lumborum*

gluteus medius*

piriformis*

gluteus maximus

ANNOTATION KEY
Black text indicates target muscles
Grey text indicates other working muscles
* indicates deep muscles

MODIFICATION
Harder: Keeping your hips on the floor, raise your arms towards the ceiling. Reach towards your toes as you lift your shoulders off the floor.

rectus femoris

iliopsoas*

obliquus externus

obliquus internus*

triceps brachii

transversus abdominis*

vastus intermedius*

tensor fasciae latae

rectus abdominis

LEG RAISE

① Lie on your back with your arms along your sides. Extend your legs and lift them off the floor, angled away from your body.

AVOID
• Relying on momentum as you lift and lower your legs.
• Using your lower back to drive the movement.
• Bending your legs.

TARGETS
• Lower abdominals

LEVEL
• Intermediate

BENEFITS
• Strengthens and tones abdominals

**NOT ADVISABLE
IF YOU HAVE . . .**
• Neck issues
• Lower-back pain

② Raise your legs until they are perpendicular to the floor.

③ Lower your legs so that your feet are just above the floor, and then raise them again, performing two sets of 20.

ANNOTATION KEY

Black text indicates target muscles

Grey text indicates other working muscles

* indicates deep muscles

DO IT RIGHT
- Keep your upper body braced.
- Use your abs to drive the movement.
- Move your legs together, as if they were a single leg.
- Keep your arms on the floor.

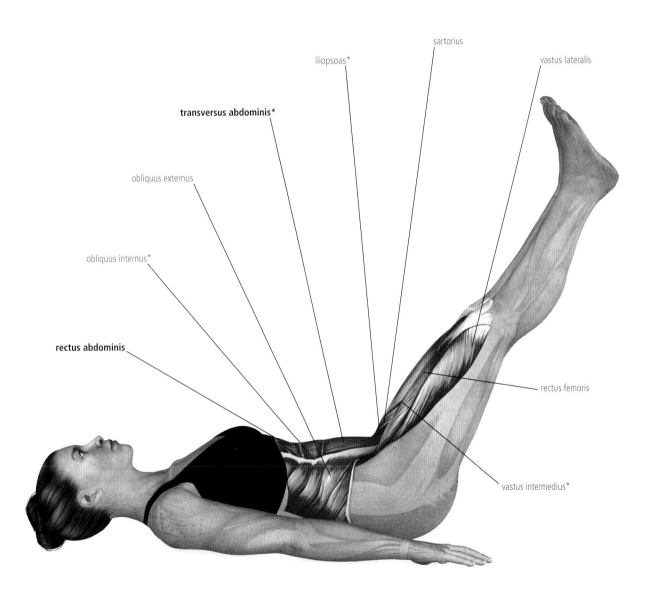

sartorius

iliopsoas*

vastus lateralis

transversus abdominis*

obliquus externus

obliquus internus*

rectus femoris

rectus abdominis

vastus intermedius*

LOWER-BODY EXERCISES

If you're like most women, a major concern is working on your lower body—trying to control those "thunder thighs" and spreading bottom. But working on your lower body doesn't just mean fitting into a pencil skirt—a conditioned lower body and strong legs can take stress off the lower back—a real bonus if you spend long days on your feet. Your gluteal muscles control your legs, hips and pelvis, and toned glutes help protect you from lower-back and lower-limb injuries. Strong thighs (the quadriceps in the front and the hamstrings at the back) allow you to walk, run, jump and squat. The major calf muscles are the gastrocnemius and the soleus. The gastrocnemius has two heads that when fully developed form a distinctive diamond shape (and give you a great set of pins).

FOAM ROLLER ILIOTIBIAL BAND RELEASE

❶ Lie on your left side, with the foam roller placed under the middle of your thigh. Support your torso with your left forearm on the floor.

❷ Bend your right leg and cross it in front of your left, so that your knee is pointed upwards. Place your right foot flat on the floor.

❸ Pulling with your shoulder and pushing with your supporting leg, roll back and forth along the side of your thigh. Adjust the placement of your arm as you make your motion bigger.

❹ Repeat 15 times on each side.

TARGETS
- Iliotibial band
- Lateral thigh muscles
- Scapular stabilisers

LEVEL
- Intermediate

BENEFITS
- Releases the iliotibial band -- this may be uncomfortable at first, but will become easier with repetition
- Strengthens the scapular stabilisers and lateral trunk muscles

NOT ADVISABLE IF YOU HAVE . . .
- Shoulder pain
- Back pain

DO IT RIGHT
- Relax your shoulders throughout the exercise.
- Press your hands and forearms firmly into the floor.

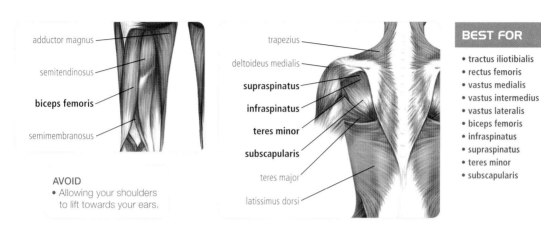

adductor magnus

semitendinosus

biceps femoris

semimembranosus

AVOID
• Allowing your shoulders to lift towards your ears.

trapezius

deltoideus medialis

supraspinatus

infraspinatus

teres minor

subscapularis

teres major

latissimus dorsi

BEST FOR

• tractus iliotibialis
• rectus femoris
• vastus medialis
• vastus intermedius
• vastus lateralis
• biceps femoris
• infraspinatus
• supraspinatus
• teres minor
• subscapularis

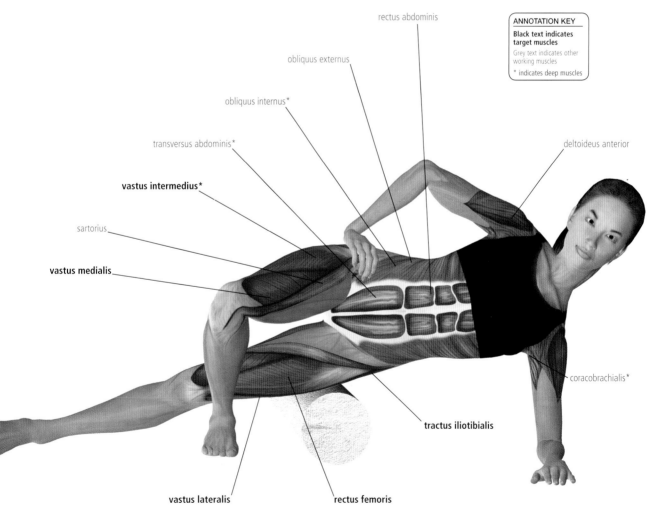

rectus abdominis

obliquus externus

obliquus internus*

transversus abdominis*

vastus intermedius*

sartorius

vastus medialis

ANNOTATION KEY
Black text indicates target muscles
Grey text indicates other working muscles
* indicates deep muscles

deltoideus anterior

coracobrachialis*

tractus iliotibialis

vastus lateralis

rectus femoris

SWISS BALL JACKKNIFE

❶ Place your hands on the floor, with your legs extended so that the tops of your feet rest on top of a Swiss ball. Keep your spine in a neutral position.

DO IT RIGHT
- Keep your chest high and retracted.
- Elongate your neck and extend your elbows throughout the movement.
- Position your hands on the floor so that they are directly below your shoulders.

❷ Flex your hips, and pull your knees in towards your chest, driving your hips upwards and retracting your abdomen.

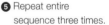

❸ Continue to pull in until your buttocks are resting on top of your heels.

❹ Hold for 5 seconds, and then extend your hips to straighten your legs and return to the starting position.

❺ Repeat entire sequence three times.

TARGETS
- Abdominals
- Hip flexors

LEVEL
- Advanced

BENEFITS
- Stabilises core
- Strengthens abdominals
- Hip flexors

NOT ADVISABLE IF YOU HAVE . . .
- Neck issues
- Lower-back pain

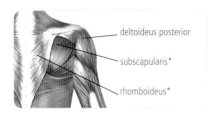

deltoideus posterior

subscapularis*

rhomboideus*

AVOID
• Bending your elbows.
• Allowing your shoulders to elevate towards your ears.

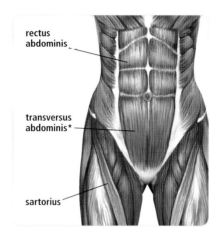

rectus abdominis

transversus abdominis*

sartorius

BEST FOR

• iliopsoas
• obliquus externus
• obliquus internus
• rectus abdominis
• sartorius
• tibialis anterior
• transversus abdominis

ANNOTATION KEY
Black text indicates target muscles
Grey text indicates other working muscles
* indicates deep muscles

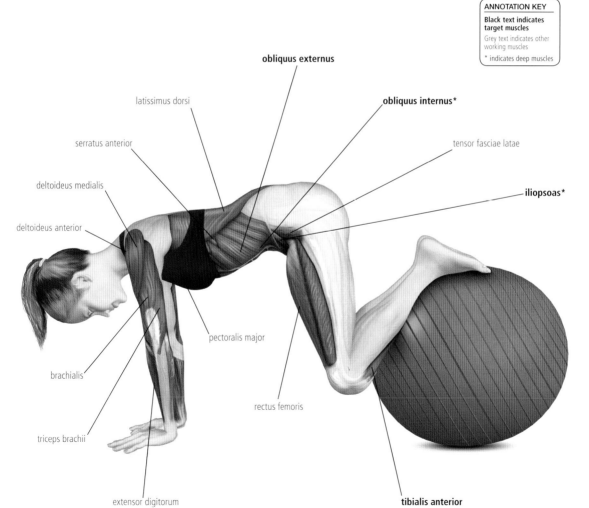

obliquus externus

latissimus dorsi

obliquus internus*

serratus anterior

tensor fasciae latae

deltoideus medialis

iliopsoas*

deltoideus anterior

pectoralis major

brachialis

rectus femoris

triceps brachii

extensor digitorum

tibialis anterior

SHOULDER BRIDGE

❶ Lie on your back with your legs bent, your feet flat on the floor, and your arms extended at your sides, angled slightly away from the body.

DO IT RIGHT
- Push through your heels, not your toes.
- Keep your knees and feet aligned.
- Keep your arms and feet on the floor.

TARGETS
- Gluteal muscles
- Hamstrings
- Quadriceps
- Lower back
- Hips

LEVEL
- Beginner

BENEFITS
- Strengthens glutes, quadriceps and hamstrings
- Stabilises core

NOT ADVISABLE IF YOU HAVE . . .
- Shoulder injury
- Neck injury
- Back injury

❷ Push through your heels while raising your glutes off the floor. With your feet and thighs parallel, push your arms into the floor, while extending through your fingertips.

❸ Lengthen your neck away from your shoulders as you lift your hips higher so that you form a straight line from shoulder to knee.

❹ Hold for 30 seconds to 1 minute. Exhale to release your spine slowly to the floor. Repeat three times.

MODIFICATION

Harder: Follow step 1 through 3, and then keeping your legs bent, bring your left knee towards your chest. Hold for 15 seconds, and then repeat on the other side.

MODIFICATION

Harder: Resting your feet on a foam roller, follow steps 2 and 3, and then elevate your right leg. Hold for 15 seconds, and then repeat on the other side.

AVOID

- Overextending your abdominals past your thighs in the finished position.
- Arching your back.

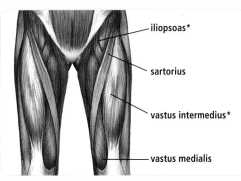

- iliopsoas*
- sartorius
- vastus intermedius*
- vastus medialis

BEST FOR

- erector spinae
- iliopsoas
- sartorius
- rectus femoris
- gluteus maximus
- gluteus medius
- gluteus minimus
- vastus lateralis
- vastus intermedius
- vastus medialis

ANNOTATION KEY

Black text indicates target muscles
Grey text indicates other working muscles
* indicates deep muscles

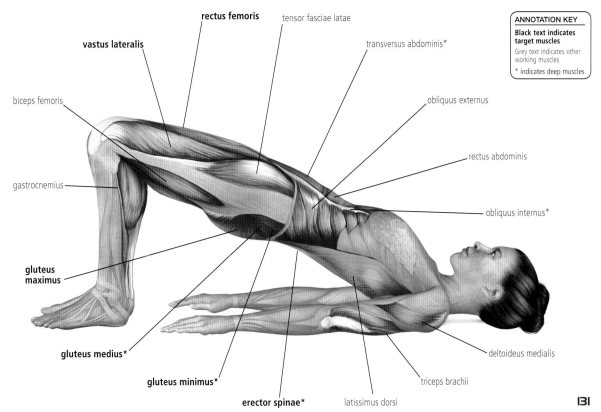

rectus femoris
tensor fasciae latae
vastus lateralis
transversus abdominis*
biceps femoris
obliquus externus
gastrocnemius
rectus abdominis
obliquus internus*
gluteus maximus
gluteus medius*
deltoideus medialis
gluteus minimus*
triceps brachii
erector spinae*
latissimus dorsi

FOAM ROLLER BICYCLE

❶ Lie on your back with a foam roller placed lengthwise under your spine, your buttocks and shoulders resting on the roller. Place your forearms on the floor on either side of the roller to balance yourself.

DO IT RIGHT
- Relax your neck throughout the exercise.
- Fully extend your leg during the downward phase of the "pedaling" movement.

❷ Draw your knees up to tabletop position, forming a 90-degree angle between your hips, thighs, and calves.

TARGETS
- Abdominals
- Quadriceps

LEVEL
- Advanced

BENEFITS
- Improves pelvic stabilisation
- Strengthens abdominals

NOT ADVISABLE IF YOU HAVE . . .
- Lower-back pain
- Neck pain

❸ Keeping your back flat, lift your head, neck and shoulders off the roller. Straighten your right leg and pull your left knee in towards your chest, keeping your head, neck and shoulders lifted.

AVOID
- Allowing your shoulders to lift towards your ears.
- Lifting your hips and lower back during the movement.

4 Switch legs while maintaining your balance, imitating the pedaling of a bicycle. Repeat 15 times on each leg.

BEST FOR

- rectus abdominis
- transversus abdominis
- obliquus internus
- obliquus externus
- triceps brachii
- vastus intermedius
- rectus femoris
- vastus medialis

ANNOTATION KEY
Black text indicates target muscles
Grey text indicates other working muscles
* indicates deep muscles

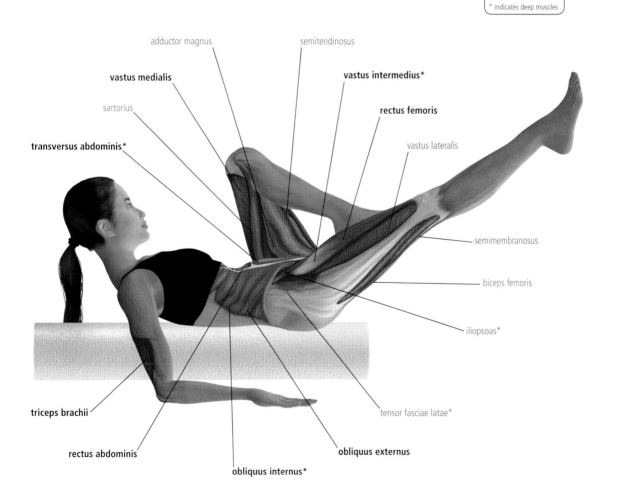

adductor magnus
semitendinosus
vastus medialis
vastus intermedius*
sartorius
rectus femoris
transversus abdominis*
vastus lateralis
semimembranosus
biceps femoris
iliopsoas*
triceps brachii
tensor fasciae latae*
rectus abdominis
obliquus externus
obliquus internus*

SINGLE-LEG CIRCLES

❶ Lie flat on the floor, with both legs and arms extended.

❷ Bend your right knee towards your chest, and then straighten your leg up in the air. Anchor the rest of your body to the floor, straightening both knees and pressing your shoulders back and down.

❸ Cross your raised leg up and over your body, aiming for your left shoulder. Continue making a circle with the raised leg, returning to the centre. Add emphasis to the motion by pausing at the top between repetitions.

TARGETS
• Pelvic stability
• Abdominals

LEVEL
• Beginner

BENEFITS
• Lengthens leg muscles
• Strengthens deep abdominal muscles

NOT ADVISABLE IF YOU HAVE . . .
• Snapping hip syndrome—if this is an issue, reduce the size of the circles.

❹ Switch directions so that you aim your leg away from your body. Repeat with the other leg. Complete full movement five to eight times.

BEST FOR

• rectus abdominis
• obliquus externus
• rectus femoris
• biceps femoris
• triceps brachii
• gluteus maximus
• adductor magnus
• vastus lateralis
• vastus medialis
• tensor fasciae latae

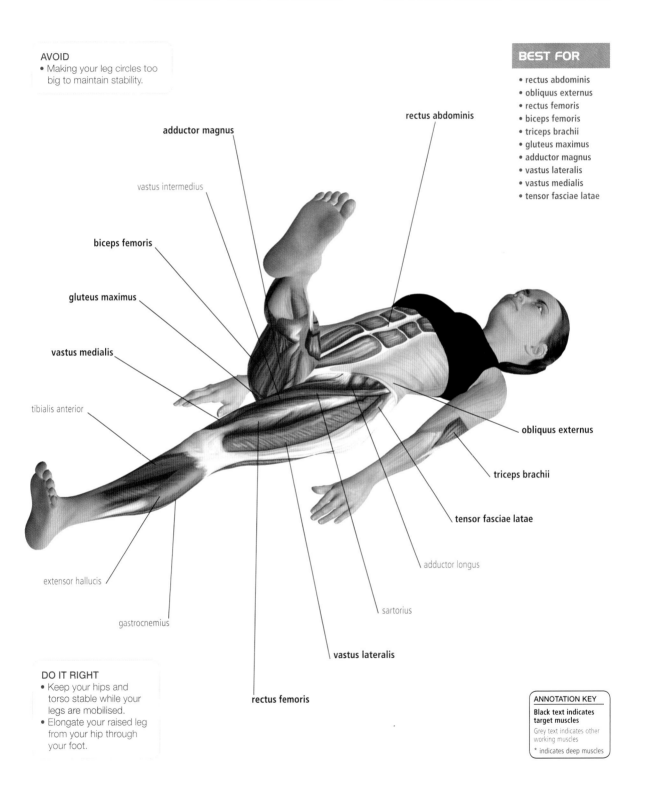

rectus abdominis

adductor magnus

vastus intermedius

biceps femoris

gluteus maximus

vastus medialis

tibialis anterior

obliquus externus

triceps brachii

tensor fasciae latae

adductor longus

extensor hallucis

sartorius

gastrocnemius

vastus lateralis

DO IT RIGHT
• Keep your hips and torso stable while your legs are mobilised.
• Elongate your raised leg from your hip through your foot.

rectus femoris

ANNOTATION KEY

Black text indicates target muscles
Grey text indicates other working muscles
* indicates deep muscles

SCISSORS

❶ Lie on your back with your knees and feet lifted in tabletop position, your thighs making a 90-degree angle with your upper body, and your arms by your sides. Inhale, drawing in your abdominals.

❷ Reach your legs straight up, and lift your head and shoulders off the floor. Hold the position while lengthening your legs.

DO IT RIGHT
- Keep your legs as straight as possible.
- Draw your navel into your spine.

❸ Stretching your right leg away from your body, raise your left leg towards your trunk. Hold your left calf with your hands, pulsing twice while keeping your shoulders down.

TARGETS
- Quadriceps
- Abdominals

LEVEL
- Intermediate

BENEFITS
- Increases stability with unilateral movement
- Increases abdominal strength and endurance

NOT ADVISABLE IF YOU HAVE . . .
- Tight hamstrings— if this is an issue, you may bend the knee that is moving towards your chest.

AVOID
- Bending your leg.

❹ Switch your legs in the air, reaching for your right leg. Stabilise your pelvis and spine. Repeat sequence six to eight times on each leg.

ANNOTATION KEY
Black text indicates target muscles
Grey text indicates other working muscles
* indicates deep muscles

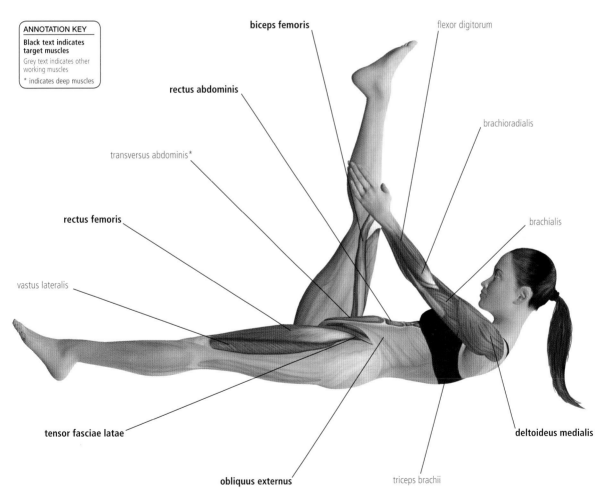

biceps femoris

flexor digitorum

rectus abdominis

transversus abdominis*

brachioradialis

rectus femoris

brachialis

vastus lateralis

tensor fasciae latae

deltoideus medialis

obliquus externus

triceps brachii

WALL SITS

DO IT RIGHT
- Keep your body firm throughout the exercise.
- Relax your shoulders and neck.
- Form a 90-degree angle with your hips and knees to receive maximum benefit from the exercise.

① Stand with your back to a wall. Lean against the wall, and walk your feet out from under your body until your lower back rests comfortably against it.

AVOID
- Sitting below 90 degrees.
- Pushing your back into the wall to hold yourself up.
- Shifting from side to side as you begin to fatigue.

TARGETS
- Quadriceps
- Gluteal muscles

LEVEL
- Beginner

BENEFITS
- Strengthens quadriceps and gluteal muscles
- Trains the body to place weight evenly between the legs

NOT ADVISABLE IF YOU HAVE . . .
- Knee pain

② Slide your torso down the wall, until your hips and knees form 90-degree angles, your thighs parallel to the floor.

③ Raise your arms straight in front of you so that they are parallel to your thighs, and relax the upper torso. Hold for 1 minute, and repeat five times.

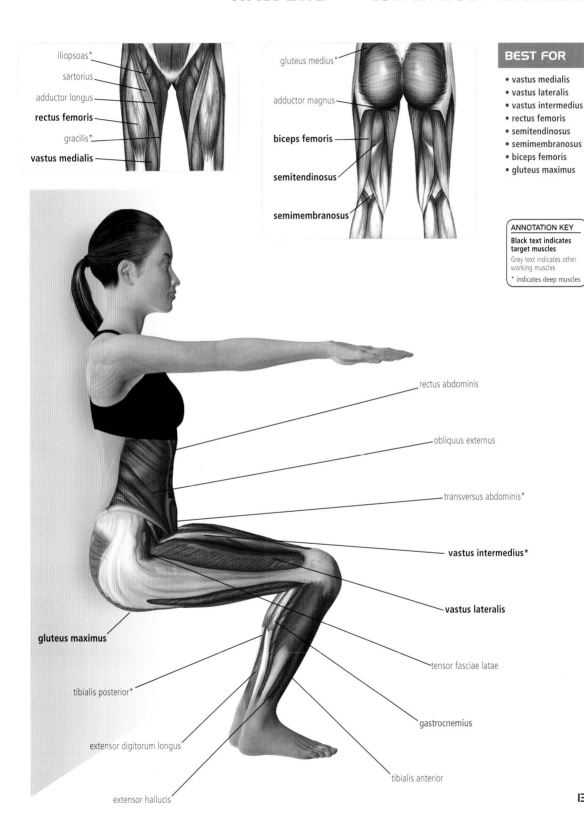

iliopsoas*
sartorius
adductor longus
rectus femoris
gracilis*
vastus medialis

gluteus medius*
adductor magnus
biceps femoris
semitendinosus
semimembranosus

BEST FOR

- vastus medialis
- vastus lateralis
- vastus intermedius
- rectus femoris
- semitendinosus
- semimembranosus
- biceps femoris
- gluteus maximus

ANNOTATION KEY

Black text indicates target muscles
Grey text indicates other working muscles
* indicates deep muscles

rectus abdominis
obliquus externus
transversus abdominis*
vastus intermedius*
vastus lateralis
tensor fasciae latae
gastrocnemius
tibialis anterior
gluteus maximus
tibialis posterior*
extensor digitorum longus
extensor hallucis

STIFF-LEGGED DEADLIFT

❶ Stand upright, feet planted about shoulder-width apart, with your arms slightly in front of your thighs with a hand weight or dumbbell in each hand. Your knees should be slightly bent and your rear pushed slightly outward.

DO IT RIGHT
- Maintain the straight line of your back.
- Keep your torso stable.
- Keep your neck straight.
- Keep your arms extended.

AVOID
- Allowing your lower back to sag or arch.
- Arching your neck, straining to look forwards while you are bent over.

TARGETS
- Back
- Buttocks
- Hamstrings

LEVEL
- Intermediate

BENEFITS
- Improves flexibility
- Stabilises lower body

NOT ADVISABLE IF YOU HAVE . . .
- Lower-back pain

❷ Keeping your back flat, hinge at the hips and bend forwards as you lower the dumbbells towards the floor. You should feel a stretch in the backs of your legs.

❸ With control, raise your upper body back to starting position. Repeat, completing three sets of 15.

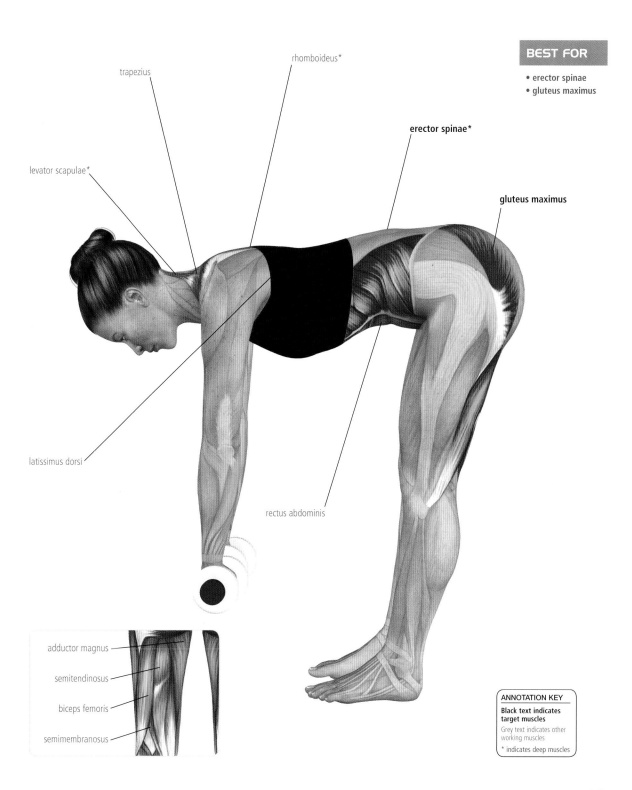

rhomboideus*

trapezius

BEST FOR
- erector spinae
- gluteus maximus

erector spinae*

levator scapulae*

gluteus maximus

latissimus dorsi

rectus abdominis

adductor magnus

semitendinosus

biceps femoris

semimembranosus

ANNOTATION KEY

Black text indicates target muscles

Grey text indicates other working muscles

* indicates deep muscles

FORWARDS LUNGE

1 Stand with your feet together and your arms hanging at your sides.

2 Exhale, and carefully step back with your right leg, keeping it in line with your hips as you step back. The ball of your left foot should be in contact with the floor as you do the motion.

3 Slowly slide your right foot farther back while bending your left knee, stacking it directly above your ankle.

4 Position your palms or fingers on the floor on either side of your left leg, and slowly press your palms or fingers against the floor to enhance the placement of your upper body and your head.

5 Lift your head and gaze straight forwards while leaning your upper body forwards and carefully rolling your shoulders down and backwards.

6 Press the ball of your right foot gradually into the floor, contract your thigh muscles, and press up to keep your left leg straight.

7 Hold for 5 seconds. Slowly return to the starting position, and then repeat on the other side.

AVOID
• Dropping your back knee to the floor.

TARGETS
• Quadriceps
• Hamstrings
• Calf muscles

LEVEL
• Beginner

BENEFITS
• Strengthens legs and arms
• Stretches groins

NOT ADVISABLE IF YOU HAVE . . .
• Arm injury
• Shoulder injury
• Hip injury
• High or low blood pressure

FORWARDS LUNGE • LOWER-BODY EXERCISES

ANNOTATION KEY

Black text indicates target muscles

Grey text indicates other working muscles

* indicates deep muscles

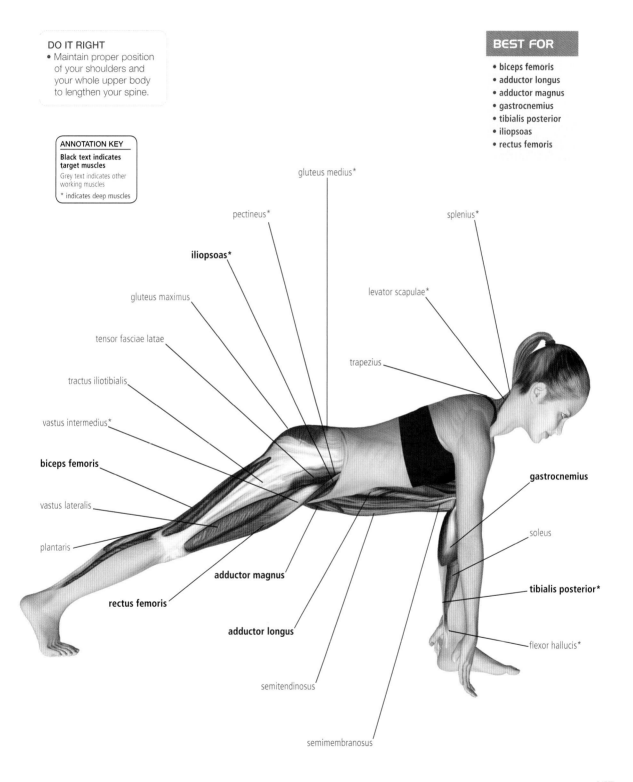

gluteus medius*

pectineus*

splenius*

iliopsoas*

levator scapulae*

gluteus maximus

tensor fasciae latae

trapezius

tractus iliotibialis

vastus intermedius*

gastrocnemius

biceps femoris

soleus

vastus lateralis

plantaris

tibialis posterior*

adductor magnus

rectus femoris

flexor hallucis*

adductor longus

semitendinosus

semimembranosus

LATERAL LUNGE

① Stand with your feet planted widely and your arms outstretched in front of you, parallel to the floor.

② Step out to the left. Squat down on your right leg, bending at your hips, while maintaining a neutral spine. Begin to extend your left leg, keeping both feet flat on the floor.

③ Bend your right knee until your thigh is parallel to the floor, and your left leg is fully extended.

④ Keeping your arms parallel to the ground, squeeze your buttocks and press off your right leg to return to the starting position, and repeat. Repeat sequence 10 times on each side.

TARGETS
- Gluteal muscles
- Quadriceps

LEVEL
- Beginner

BENEFITS
- Strengthens the pelvic, trunk and knee stabilisers

NOT ADVISABLE IF YOU HAVE . . .
- Knee pain
- Back pain
- Trouble bearing weight on one leg

DO IT RIGHT
- Keep your spine in neutral position as you bend your hips.
- Relax your shoulders and neck.
- Align your knee with the toe of your bent leg.
- Tighten your glutes as you bend.

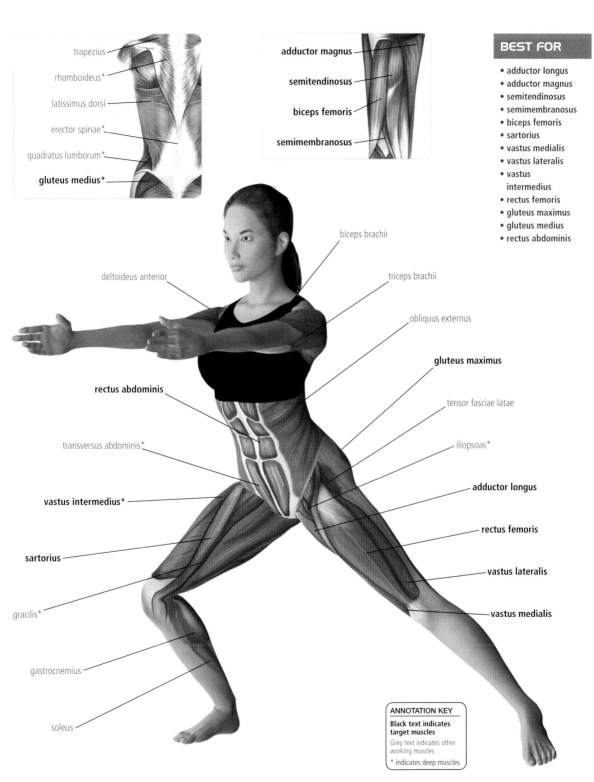

trapezius

rhomboideus*

latissimus dorsi

erector spinae*

quadratus lumborum*

gluteus medius*

adductor magnus

semitendinosus

biceps femoris

semimembranosus

BEST FOR

- adductor longus
- adductor magnus
- semitendinosus
- semimembranosus
- biceps femoris
- sartorius
- vastus medialis
- vastus lateralis
- vastus intermedius
- rectus femoris
- gluteus maximus
- gluteus medius
- rectus abdominis

biceps brachii

deltoideus anterior

triceps brachii

obliquus externus

gluteus maximus

rectus abdominis

tensor fasciae latae

transversus abdominis*

iliopsoas*

adductor longus

vastus intermedius*

rectus femoris

sartorius

vastus lateralis

gracilis*

vastus medialis

gastrocnemius

soleus

ANNOTATION KEY

Black text indicates target muscles

Grey text indicates other working muscles

* indicates deep muscles

DUMBBELL LUNGE

❶ Stand with your feet planted about shoulder-width apart, with your arms at your sides and a hand weight or dumbbell in each hand.

DO IT RIGHT
- Keep your body facing forwards as you step one leg in front of you.
- Stand upright.
- Gaze forwards.
- Ease into the lunge.
- Make sure that your front knee is facing forwards.

AVOID
- Turning your body to one side.
- Allowing your knee to extend past your foot.
- Arching your back.

TARGETS
- Gluteal muscles
- Quadriceps

LEVEL
- Intermediate

BENEFITS
- Strengthens and tones quadriceps and glutes

NOT ADVISABLE IF YOU HAVE . . .
- Knee issues

❷ Keeping your head up and your spine neutral, take a big step forwards.

BEST FOR
- gluteus maximus
- rectus femoris
- vastus lateralis
- vastus intermedius
- vastus medialis

3 In one movement as you step forwards, bend your front knee to a 90-degree angle, and drop your front thigh until it is parallel to the floor. Your back knee will drop behind you so that you are balancing on the toe of your back foot, creating a straight line from your spine to the back of your knee.

4 Push through your front heel to stand upright, and then return to starting position. Repeat on the other leg, alternating to perform three sets of 15 lunges per leg.

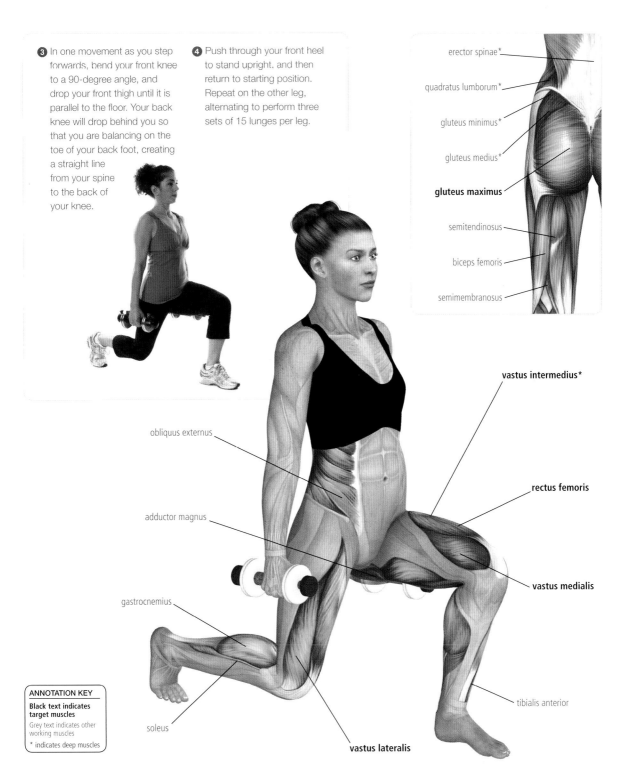

erector spinae*

quadratus lumborum*

gluteus minimus*

gluteus medius*

gluteus maximus

semitendinosus

biceps femoris

semimembranosus

obliquus externus

adductor magnus

gastrocnemius

soleus

vastus intermedius*

rectus femoris

vastus medialis

tibialis anterior

vastus lateralis

ANNOTATION KEY

Black text indicates target muscles

Grey text indicates other working muscles

* indicates deep muscles

DUMBBELL CALF RAISE

❶ Stand with your arms at your sides, holding a hand weight or dumbbell in each hand with palms facing inward.

❷ Keeping the rest of your body steady, slowly raise your heels off the floor to balance on the balls of your feet.

❸ Hold for 10 seconds, lower, and repeat, performing three sets of 15.

TARGETS
• Calves

LEVEL
• Intermediate

BENEFITS
• Strengthens calf muscles

NOT ADVISABLE IF YOU HAVE . . .
• Ankle issues

DO IT RIGHT
• Keep your legs straight.
• Concentrate on the contraction in your calves as you balance on the balls of your feet; to feel a greater contraction, rise higher.
• Keep your core stable and your back straight.
• Gaze forwards.
• Try to balance on the balls of your feet.

DUMBBELL CALF RAISE • LOWER-BODY EXERCISES

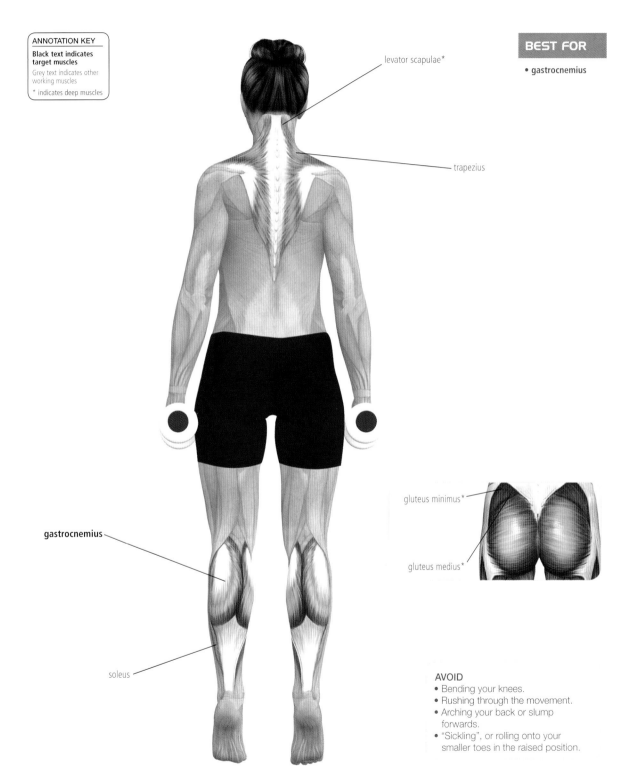

ANNOTATION KEY

Black text indicates target muscles

Grey text indicates other working muscles

* indicates deep muscles

levator scapulae*

trapezius

BEST FOR

• gastrocnemius

gluteus minimus*

gluteus medius*

gastrocnemius

soleus

AVOID
• Bending your knees.
• Rushing through the movement.
• Arching your back or slump forwards.
• "Sickling", or rolling onto your smaller toes in the raised position.

KNEELING SIDE LIFT

1 Kneel with your right leg outstretched to the side and your left leg lined up under your hips. Place both hands behind your head, with your elbows extended out to the sides.

AVOID
• Sinking into your neck or shoulders.

2 Begin leaning your torso to the left.

TARGETS
• Abductor muscles
• Abdominals
• Gluteal muscles

LEVEL
• Advanced

BENEFITS
• Trims the waistline

NOT ADVISABLE IF YOU HAVE . . .
• Knee issues
• Back pain

3 Lift your right leg off the floor, bringing it as high as your hips. Repeat sequence five to six times. Switch sides, and repeat the sequence with your left leg.

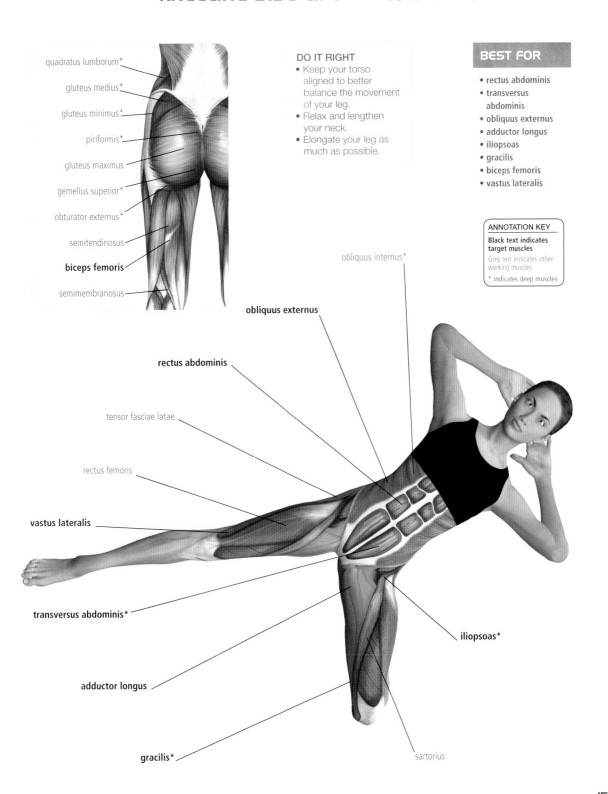

quadratus lumborum*

gluteus medius*

gluteus minimus*

piriformis*

gluteus maximus

gemellus superior*

obturator externus*

semitendinosus

biceps femoris

semimembranosus

DO IT RIGHT
- Keep your torso aligned to better balance the movement of your leg.
- Relax and lengthen your neck.
- Elongate your leg as much as possible.

BEST FOR
- rectus abdominis
- transversus abdominis
- obliquus externus
- adductor longus
- iliopsoas
- gracilis
- biceps femoris
- vastus lateralis

ANNOTATION KEY

Black text indicates target muscles

Grey text indicates other working muscles

* indicates deep muscles

obliquus internus*

obliquus externus

rectus abdominis

tensor fasciae latae

rectus femoris

vastus lateralis

transversus abdominis*

adductor longus

iliopsoas*

gracilis*

sartorius

PUT IT ALL TOGETHER:
WORKOUTS

Once you have gone through the exercises in this book and practised executing them properly, your next step is to put these moves together into workouts. The following sequences present a sample of the many ways you can combine these exercises to target varying aims, whether you are a beginner just setting out on your first fitness programme or a seasoned exerciser with a specific goal, such as whittling your waistline. Keep in mind that the sequence lists really just provide you with flexible frameworks—if you want to avoid a certain exercise in any one of them, simply substitute another that has a similar benefit. After trying the workouts featured here, flip through the exercises and create your own workouts to suit your individual fitness goals.

BEGINNER'S WORKOUT

A balanced introductory sequence for the exercise novice, but this workout also benefits anyone of any level.

① Chest Stretch — page 20
② Iliotibial Band Stretch — page 36
③ Dumbbell Upright Row — pages 66–67
④ Alternating Dumbbell Curl — pages 68–69
⑤ Forward Lunge — pages 142–143
⑥ Lateral Lunge — pages 144–145
⑦ Half Curl — pages 74–75
⑧ Swiss Ball Sitting Balance — pages 114–115
⑨ Swiss Ball Hip Circles — pages 116–117
⑩ Tiny Steps — pages 102–103
⑪ Shoulder Bridge — pages 130–131
⑫ Piriformis Stretch — page 28

BACK TO BASICS

Some things never go out of style—such as this workout featuring some tried-and-true exercise staples.

① Triceps Stretch — page 17
② Shoulder Bridge — pages 130–131
③ Single-Leg Circles — pages 134–135
④ Scissors — pages 136–137
⑤ Crunch — pages 72–73
⑥ Plank — pages 90–91
⑦ Push-Up — pages 62–63
⑧ Child's Pose — pages 40–41

LEANER LEGS, THIGHS & GLUTES

With its focus on strengthening your abs, glutes and legs, this workout will get you into your favourite jeans.

1 Hip-to-Thigh Stretch
page 30

2 Quadriceps Stretch
page 37

3 Standing Hamstrings Stretch
page 38

4 Standing Calf Stretch
page 39

5 Wall Sits
pages 138–139

6 Forward Lunge
pages 142–143

7 Lateral Lunge
pages 144–145

8 Dumbbell Lunge
pages 146–147

9 Dumbbell Calf Raise
pages 148–149

10 Stiff-Legged Deadlift
pages 140–141

11 Kneeling Side Lift
pages 150–151

12 Foam Roller Bicycle
pages 132–133

ARM TONER

Practise this workout regularly, and you'll soon be showing off toned arms in sleeveless tops and dresses.

1 Chair Dip
pages 44–45

2 Overhead Press
pages 48–49

3 Alternating Chest Press
pages 50–51

4 Standing Fly
pages 52–53

5 Swiss Ball Pullover
pages 56–57

6 Swiss Ball Triceps Extension
pages 58–59

7 Swiss Ball Fly
pages 60–61

8 Alternating Dumbbell Curl
pages 68-69

CORE STRENGTH & STABILITY

Working the core is one of the surest ways to get fit and strong, so you'll look and feel your best.

1 Half Curl — pages 74–75

2 The Boat — pages 84–85

3 V-Up — pages 86–87

4 Backwards Ball Stretch — pages 88–89

5 Swiss Ball Transverse Abs — pages 92–93

6 Swiss Ball Rollout — pages 94–95

7 Foam Roller Calf Press — pages 96–97

8 Foam Roller Diagonal Crunch — pages 98–99

9 Foam Roller Supine Marches — pages 100–101

10 Tiny Steps — pages 102–103

11 Abdominal Hip Lift — pages 120–121

12 Leg Raise — pages 122–123

WORKING THE WAISTLINE

A focus on the obliques will help you trim and tone your midsection and take inches off your waist.

1 Seated Russian Twist — pages 76–77

2 Spine Twist — pages 78–79

3 Oblique Roll-Down — pages 80–81

4 Bicycle Crunch — pages 82–83

5 Swiss Ball Hip Crossover — pages 32–33

6 Swiss Ball Reverse Bridge Rotation — pages 112–113

7 Swiss Ball Hip Circles — pages 116–117

8 Swiss Ball Reverse Bridge Roll — pages 118–119

ALL-OVER TONING

This is a great plan for getting a full-body workout that helps you achieve maximum performance levels.

1 Posterior Hand Clasp — pages 18–19

2 Swiss Ball Kneeling Lat Stretch — page 21

3 Prone Trunk Raise — pages 64–65

4 Chair Dip — pages 44–45

5 Chair Crunch — pages 46–47

6 Double-Leg Abdominal Press — page 104–105

7 The Twist — pages 106–107

8 Standing Knee Crunch — pages 108–109

9 Power Squat — 110–111

10 Foam Roller Iliotibial Band Release — pages 126–127

11 Swiss Ball Jackknife — pages 128–129

12 Upward Plank — pages 54–55

STRETCH IT OUT

Give your back a soothing stretch with this quick flexibility workout that takes less than 10 minutes.

1 Neck Side Bend — page 16

2 Latissimus Dorsi Stretch — pages 22–23

3 Toe Touch — pages 24–25

4 Cat and Dog Stretch — pages 26–27

5 Hip Stretch — page 29

6 Spine Stretch — page 31

7 Knee-to-Chest Hug — pages 34–35

8 Child's Pose — pages 40–41

GLOSSARY

GENERAL TERMS

abduction: Movement away from the body.

adduction: Movement towards the body.

anterior: Located in the front.

cardiovascular exercise: Any exercise that increases the heart rate, making oxygen and nutrient-rich blood available to working muscles.

core: Refers to the deep muscle layers that lie close to the spine and provide structural support for the entire body. The core is divisible into two groups: major core and minor core muscles. The major muscles reside on the trunk and include the belly area and the mid and lower back. This area encompasses the pelvic floor muscles (levator ani, pubococcygeus, iliococcygeus, puborectalis and coccygeus), the abdominals (rectus abdominis, transversus abdominis, obliquus externus and obliquus internus), the spinal extensors (multifidus spinae, erector spinae, splenius, longissimus thoracis, and semispinalis), and the diaphragm. The minor core muscles include the latissimus dorsi, gluteus maximus and trapezius (upper, middle and lower). Minor core muscles assist the major core muscles when the body engages in activities or movements that require added stability.

crunch: A common abdominal exercise that calls for curling the shoulders towards the pelvis while lying supine with hands behind the head and knees bent.

curl: An exercise movement, usually targeting the biceps brachii, that calls for a weight to be moved through an arc, in a "curling" motion.

deadlift: An exercise movement that calls for lifting a weight, such as a dumbbell, off the floor from a stabilised bent-over position.

dumbbell: A basic piece of equipment that consists of a short bar on which plates are secured. A person can use a dumbbell in one hand or both hands during an exercise. Most gyms and fitness centres offer dumbbells with the weight plates welded on and poundage indicated on the plates, but many dumbbells intended for home use come with removable plates that allow you to adjust the weight.

extension: The act of straightening.

extensor muscle: A muscle serving to extend a body part away from the body.

flexion: The bending of a joint.

flexor muscle: A muscle that decreases the angle between two bones, as when bending the arm at the elbow or raising the thigh toward the stomach.

fly: An exercise movement in which the hand and arm move through an arc while the elbow is kept at a constant angle. Flyes work the muscles of the upper body.

Foam roller: A firm tube of dense foam used for stretching and strengthening exercises, balance and stability training and self-massage. Providing similar benefits as deep-tissue massage, rollers come in a variety of sizes, materials and densities.

hand weight: Any of a range of free weights that are often used in weight training and toning. Small hand weights are usually cast iron formed in the shape of a dumbbell, sometimes coated with rubber or neoprene for comfort.

iliotibial band (ITB): A thick band of fibrous tissue that runs down the outside of the leg, beginning at the hip and extending to the outer side of the tibia just below the knee joint. The band functions in concert with several of the thigh muscles to provide stability to the outside of the knee joint.

lateral: Located on, or extending towards, the outside.

medial: Located on, or extending towards, the middle.

medicine ball: A small weighted ball used in weight training and toning.

neutral position (spine): A spinal position resembling an S shape, consisting of a inward curve in the lower back, when viewed in profile.

posterior: Located behind.

press: An exercise movement that calls for moving a weight or other resistance away from the body.

range of motion: The distance and direction a joint can move between the flexed position and the extended position.

resistance band: Any rubber tubing or flat band device that provides a resistive force used for strength training. Also called a "fitness band", "Thera-Band", "Dyna-Band", "stretching band" and "exercise band."

rotator muscle: One of a group of muscles that assist the rotation of a joint, such as the hip or the shoulder.

scapula: The protrusion of bone on the mid to upper back, also known as the "shoulder blade".

squat: An exercise movement that calls for moving the hips back and bending the knees and hips to lower the torso and an accompanying weight, and then returning to the upright position. A squat primarily targets the muscles of the thighs, hips and buttocks, and hamstrings.

Swiss ball: A flexible, inflatable PVC ball measuring approximately 30 to 75 centimetres in circumference that is used for weight training, physical therapy, balance training and many other exercise programmes. It is also called a "balance ball", "fitness ball", "stability ball", "exercise ball", "gym ball", "physioball", "body ball" and many other names.

warm-up: Any form of light exercise of short duration that prepares the body for more intense exercises.

weight: Refers to the plates or weight stacks, or the actual poundage listed on the bar or dumbbell.

LATIN TERMS

The following glossary explains the Latin terms used to describe the muscles of the human body. Certain words are derived from Greek, which is indicated in each instance.

CHEST

coracobrachialis: Greek *korakoeidés*, "ravenlike", and *brachium*, "arm"

pectoralis (major and minor): *pectus*, "breast"

ABDOMEN

obliquus externus: *obliquus*, "slanting", and *externus*, "outwards"

obliquus internus: *obliquus*, "slanting", and *internus*, "within"

rectus abdominis: *rego*, "straight, upright", and *abdomen*, "belly"

serratus anterior: *serra*, "saw", and *ante*, "before"

transversus abdominis: *transversus*, "athwart", and *abdomen*, "belly"

NECK

scalenus: Greek *skalénós*, "unequal"

semispinalis: *semi*, "half", and *spinae*, "spine"

splenius: Greek *splénion*, "plaster, patch"

sternocleidomastoideus: Greek *stérnon*, "chest", Greek *kleis*, "key", and Greek *mastoeidés*, "breastlike"

BACK

erector spinae: *erectus*, "straight", and *spina*, "thorn"

latissimus dorsi: *latus*, "wide", and *dorsum*, "back"

multifidus spinae: *multifid*, "to cut into divisions", and *spinae*, "spine"

quadratus lumborum: *quadratus*, "square, rectangular", and *lumbus*, "loin"

rhomboideus: Greek *rhembesthai*, "to spin"

trapezius: Greek *trapezion*, "small table"

SHOULDERS

deltoideus (anterior, medial, and posterior): Greek *deltoeidés*, "delta-shaped"

infraspinatus: *infra*, "under", and *spina*, "thorn"

levator scapulae: *levare*, "to raise", and *scapulae*, "shoulder [blades]"

subscapularis: *sub*, "below", and *scapulae*, "shoulder [blades]"

supraspinatus: *supra*, "above", and *spina*, "thorn"

teres (major and minor): *teres*, "rounded"

UPPER ARM

biceps brachii: *biceps*, "two-headed", and *brachium*, "arm"

brachialis: *brachium*, "arm"

triceps brachii: *triceps*, "three-headed", and *brachium*, "arm"

LOWER ARM

anconeus: Greek *anconad*, "elbow"

brachioradialis: *brachium*, "arm", and *radius*, "spoke"

extensor carpi radialis: *extendere*, "to extend", Greek *karpós*, "wrist", and *radius*, "spoke"

extensor digitorum: *extendere*, "to extend", and *digitus*, "finger, toe"

flexor carpi pollicis longus: *flectere*, "to bend", Greek *karpós*, "wrist", *pollicis*, "thumb", and *longus*, "long"

flexor carpi radialis: *flectere*, "to bend", Greek *karpós*, "wrist", and *radius*, "spoke"

flexor carpi ulnaris: *flectere*, "to bend", Greek *karpós*, "wrist", and *ulnaris*, "forearm"

flexor digitorum: *flectere*, "to bend", and *digitus*, "finger, toe"

palmaris longus: *palmaris*, "palm," and *longus*, "long"

pronator teres: *pronate*, "to rotate", and *teres*, "rounded"

HIPS

gemellus (inferior and superior): *geminus*, "twin"

gluteus maximus: Greek *gloutós*, "rump", and *maximus*, "largest"

gluteus medius: Greek *gloutós*, "rump", and *medialis*, "middle"

gluteus minimus: Greek *gloutós*, "rump", and *minimus*, "smallest"

iliopsoas: *ilium*, "groin", and Greek *psoa*, "groin muscle"

iliacus: *ilium*, "groin"

obturator externus: *obturare*, "to block", and *externus*, "outwards"

obturator internus: *obturare*, "to block", and *internus*, "within"

pectineus: *pectin*, "comb"

piriformis: *pirum*, "pear", and *forma*, "shape"

quadratus femoris: *quadratus*, "square, rectangular", and *femur*, "thigh"

UPPER LEG

adductor longus: *adducere*, "to contract", and *longus*, "long"

adductor magnus: *adducere*, "to contract", and *magnus*, "major"

biceps femoris: *biceps*, "two-headed", and *femur*, "thigh"

gracilis: *gracilis*, "slim, slender"

rectus femoris: *rego*, "straight, upright", and *femur*, "thigh"

sartorius: *sarcio*, "to patch" or "to repair"

semimembranosus: *semi*, "half", and *membrum*, "limb"

semitendinosus: *semi*, "half", and *tendo*, "tendon"

tensor fasciae latae: *tenere*, "to stretch", *fasciae*, "band", and *latae*, "laid down"

vastus intermedius: *vastus*, "immense, huge", and *intermedius*, "between"

vastus lateralis: *vastus*, "immense, huge", and *lateralis*, "side"

vastus medialis: *vastus*, "immense, huge", and *medialis*, "middle"

LOWER LEG

adductor digiti minimi: *adducere*, "to contract", *digitus*, "finger, toe", and *minimum* "smallest"

adductor hallucis: *adducere*, "to contract", and *hallex*, "big toe"

extensor digitorum: *extendere*, "to extend", and *digitus*, "finger, toe"

extensor hallucis: *extendere*, "to extend", and *hallex*, "big toe"

flexor digitorum: *flectere*, "to bend", and *digitus*, "finger, toe"

flexor hallucis: *flectere*, "to bend", and *hallex*, "big toe"

gastrocnemius: Greek *gastroknémia*, "calf"

peroneus: *peronei*, "of the fibula"

plantaris: *planta*, "the sole"

soleus: *solea*, "sandal"

tibialis anterior: *tibia*, "reed pipe", and *ante*, "before"

tibialis posterior: *tibia*, "reed pipe", and *posterus*, "coming after"

CREDITS & ACKNOWLEDGEMENTS

All photographs by Jonathan Conklin/Jonathan Conklin Photography, Inc. (http://jonathanconklin.net/), except the following: page 11 top left Serg64/ Shutterstock.com, and top middle picamaniac/Shutterstock.com.

Models: Elaine Altholz, Goldie Oren, and Melissa Grant

All large anatomical illustrations by Hector Aiza/3D Labz Animation India (www.3dlabz.com), with small insets by Linda Bucklin/Shutterstock.com

Acknowledgements

The author and publisher also offer thanks to those closely involved in the creation of this book: Moseley Road president Sean Moore; production designer Adam Moore; designers Danielle Scaramuzzo and Terasa Bernard; and photographer Jonathan Conklin.